new to **cooking**

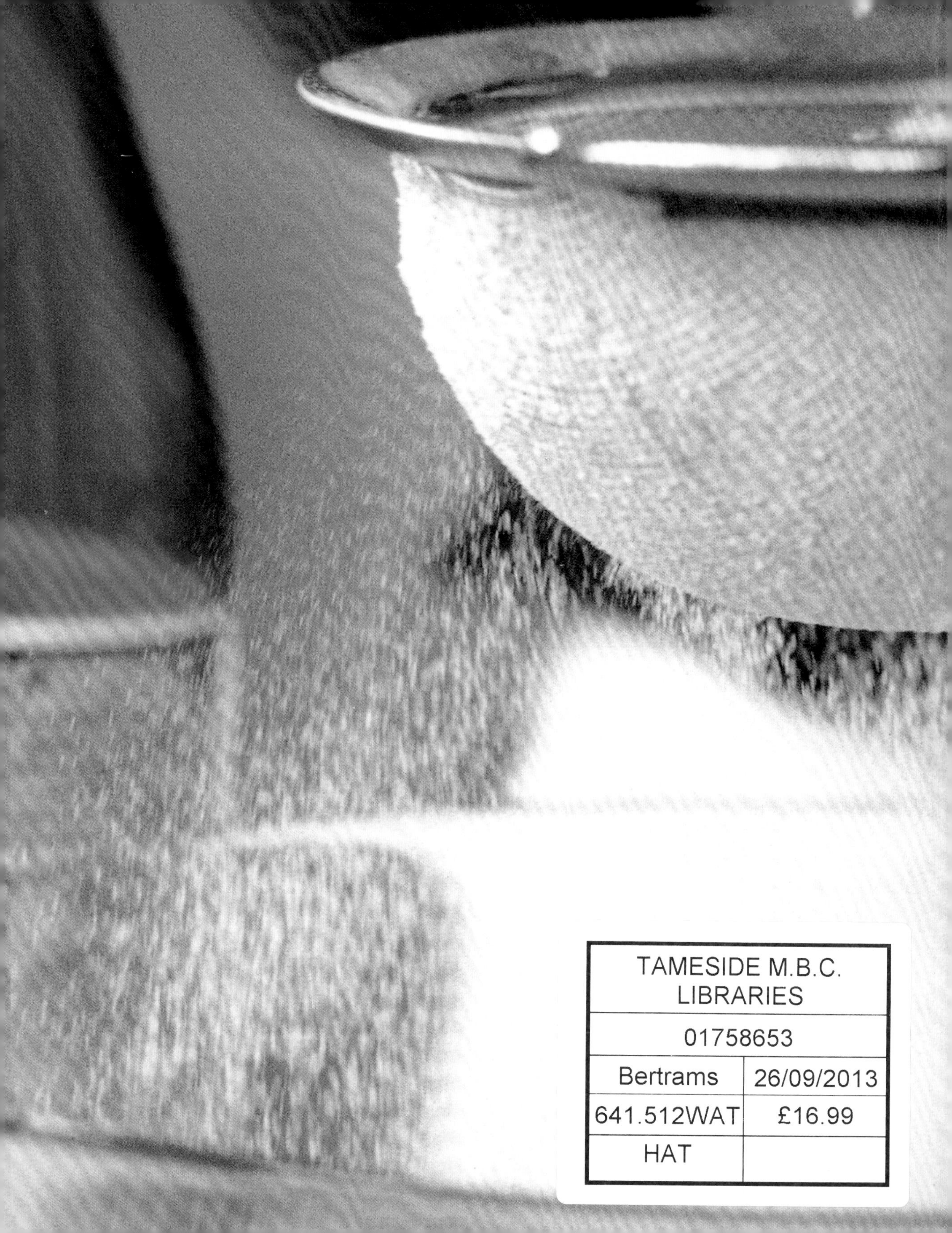

new
to **cooking**

simple skills and great recipes
for the first-time cook

lesley waters

photography by **peter cassidy**

RYLAND PETERS & SMALL
LONDON • NEW YORK

Designer Julie Bennett
Editors Sally Somers and Céline Hughes
Production Gordana Simakovic
Art Director Leslie Harrington
Editorial Director Julia Charles

Food Stylist Julz Beresford
Assistant Food Stylist Annalisa Aldridge
Stylist Helen Trent
Photographer's Assistant Rachel Tomlinson
Indexer Hilary Bird

Originally published in 2001
This edition published in 2013
by Ryland Peters & Small
20–21 Jockey's Fields
London WC1R 4BW
and
519 Broadway, 5th Floor
New York, NY 10012
www.rylandpeters.com

10 9 8 7 6 5 4 3 2 1

Text © Lesley Waters 2001, 2013

Design and photographs
© Ryland Peters & Small 2001, 2013

The author's moral rights have been asserted.

ISBN 978-1-84975-460-6

A CIP record for this book is available from the
British Library.

The original edition is cataloged as follows:
Library of Congress Cataloging-in-Publication Data

Waters, Lesley.
    How to cook / Lesley Waters ; photography by
    Peter Cassidy.
        p. cm.
    Includes index.
    ISBN 1-84172-207-3
    1. Quick and easy cookery. I. Title.

    TX833.5 .W38 2001
    641.5'55--dc21   2001031885

Printed and bound in China

Notes

All spoon measurements are level unless otherwise
noted.

All fruit and vegetables should be washed thoroughly
and peeled in the usual way, unless otherwise
advised.

Unwaxed citrus fruits and cucumbers should
be used wherever possible.

Soft cheeses and uncooked or partly cooked eggs
should not be served to the very old or frail, the very
young or to pregnant women.

Ovens should be preheated to the specified
temperature. Recipes in this book were tested with a
fan-assisted oven. If using a regular oven, increase
the cooking times according to the manufacturer's
instructions.

The publisher and author would like to thank
the following companies and stores who loaned
the glassware, plates, bowls, cutlery, table linen
and accessories that appear in the book:

Purves & Purves
www.purves.co.uk

The Conran Shop
81 Fulham Road
London SW6 6RD
www.conranshop.co.uk

Heal's
196 Tottenham Court Road
London W1T 7LQ
www.heals.co.uk

Dedication

For Barbara and Mac

Author's acknowledgments

Many thanks to my friends, neighbours and
family who chomped their way through this
book. To Sally Somers for patiently (and
politely!) checking and rechecking and
for Peter Cassidy's thoroughly modern and
fresh approach to the photography. Last,
but certainly not least, Annalisa Aldridge
and Emma Marsden for their hard work and
dedication in the kitchen.

contents

good food is for every day...

I meet a lot of people who want to cook but don't know how or are too scared to enter the kitchen in case they make a mistake. To me, the most important things about cooking are confidence, enjoyment and not being afraid to make mistakes. In fact, they can often be put right to give even better results – some of the best recipes started life by accident!

I have been cooking for over twenty years now, and for eight of those I was a cookery teacher. Of all the work I've ever done – whether it was writing books or presenting on TV, or working in a restaurant – this was my most fulfilling time. Seeing people become liberated in a kitchen was so exciting, and giving them the confidence to make lovely food was just such a pleasure.

My dream has always been to have a cookery school – and now I do! I heard someone say the other day, "Good is simple, simple is good", which sums up perfectly how I feel about food and the way it is now.

When I was training to be a chef, many of the recipes were very, very complicated and often rich and over garnished. Since then my style of food has changed dramatically. I believe that good food is for every day and not once every two weeks for a dinner party. Don't put this book on the shelf and dip into it only once in a while – use it every day! To me, real cookbooks are those which are well thumbed and splattered with ingredients.

This is the book that will teach you the skills that you will use every day, without unnecessary complications. I'll teach you how to make simple bread but tell you to buy the sponge fingers/ladyfingers to go in your Peach Marsala Trifle – life really is too short, and cutting a few corners doesn't have to mean compromising on taste.

New to Cooking will show you how to have fun and success in the kitchen. The opening chapter is dedicated to essential utensils and important storecupboard ingredients. Next are the chapters which teach you the basic techniques – from poaching, steaming and baking to roasting and grilling/broiling – all illustrated with modern recipes to guide you along the way.

I know it's tempting to go straight to the recipes and to get cooking, but do read the tips at the beginning of all the "Basics" chapters first – they contain lots of essential information.

Once you've got all the basics under your belt, the second part of the book is graduation time, with fabulous recipes for you to put the skills into practice.

I'm often asked what my favourite style of food is and it's always a difficult question to answer. All I can say is that I've been inspired by all the different people I have met and the places I have been – they have all contributed to the way I cook and eat now. I hope this book can be the beginning of your inspiration.

the kitchen

On these pages is a simple list of essential equipment and storecupboard basics and how to store them. If you already have some of these items, take all your equipment out of the cupboards and drawers and lay it on the table. Then check the tools list to see if you have everything, and put it in its place. If there's any equipment left on the table and you haven't used it in the last 12 months, give it to a friend or to a charity. As funds allow, try to assemble all the equipment in the Startup Kit. For Christmas and birthdays, perhaps your friends can be persuaded to give you the items on the Wish List.

The storecupboard is the backbone of your cooking and enables you to be spontaneous in the kitchen. There are many dishes that can be prepared using storecupboard basics. However, being well stocked doesn't mean bulk-buying. It means choosing ingredients which you will need on an everyday basis.

As well as a stock of basics such as beans, pasta and rice, it's also a good idea to keep your favourite flavourings, to turn something ordinary into something special.

tools and utensils

Startup kit
For a basic set of equipment, buy the best you can afford, then they'll last.

In your cupboards
1 non-stick frying pan
1 non-stick wok with lid
1 heavy shallow pan with ovenproof handles for stove-top or oven cooking
3 saucepans – small, medium and very large – with lids
1 collapsible metal steamer, bamboo steamer or 2-tier steaming saucepan
1 wire rack
1 handheld blender
1 sieve/strainer
1 colander with legs or stand
1 box grater
1 set of plastic bowls

1 measuring jug/set of cups
1 lemon squeezer
1 salad spinner

On the shelf
1 set of measuring scales
salt and pepper mills
1 cafetière and/or 1 teapot

In a block or wrap
1 paring or utility knife
1 large chopping knife
1 bread knife
1 pair kitchen scissors
1 sharpening steel

On the work surface
1 heavy wooden chopping/ cutting board
1 white heavy plastic board for raw meat and fish
1 roll of kitchen paper/ paper towels

In a large utensil pot
2 wooden spoons
1 large metal spoon
1 large slotted metal spoon
1 ladle
1 potato masher
1 long handled turner (fish slice)
2 plastic spatulas
1 set salad servers
1 pair of tongs

In the top drawer
1 potato peeler
1 can opener
1 corkscrew
2 metal skewers
1 rolling pin

In the bottom drawer
greaseproof paper
aluminium foil
microwave-safe clingfilm/ plastic wrap

1 roll medium freezer bags
1 roll of large heavy-duty black bin bags
1 roll of kitchen twine
dish towels
apron
oven gloves/mitts

For the oven
1 non-stick roasting pan
12-hole non-stick muffin pan
1 non-stick baking sheet

Wish list:
In your cupboards
1 food processor
1 electric mixer
1 stove-top grill pan
6 ramekin dishes (150 ml/⅔ cup)
3 glass bowls – small, medium and large
1 rolling pin

1 cooking thermometer
1 olive oil drizzler
1 mortar and pestle
1 mini blender

In a large utensil pot
extra wooden spoons
1 metal whisk
1 palette knife
1 meshed spoon for
  deep-frying

In the top drawer
parchment paper
1 roll large freezer bags
1 pastry brush

In the bottom drawer
more dish towels (12 total)
another apron
another set of oven
  gloves/ mitts

For the oven
another roasting pan
1 loose-bottomed tart pan
  (25 cm/10 inch diameter)
1 non-stick springform
  cake pan (20 cm/8 inch
  diameter)
1 cake pan (18 cm/8 inch
  square)
another non-stick
  baking sheet

storecupboard basics

Startup kit
For every day, when there's
just you, cook whatever you
fancy and serve it however
you wish.

Staples
2–3 bags pasta, various
  shapes
2–3 bags rice – long grain,
  basmati, Thai fragrant,
  risotto
egg or rice noodles
dried lentils (Puy are my
  favourites)
plain/all-purpose and
  self-raising flour
baking powder
coffee, tea and sugar

Cans and cartons
vegetable bouillon (stock)
chicken bouillon (stock)
cans of: chopped tomatoes,
  chickpeas, cannellini
  and borlotti beans,
  anchovies in oil
coconut cream or milk

Oils and vinegars
large bottles of olive oil and
  sunflower oil

small bottles of extra virgin
  olive oil for salads,
  peanut oil for frying,
  chilli/chili oil for flavour
balsamic vinegar
Worcestershire sauce
red and white wine vinegar

Spices
whole nutmegs
ground cumin
ground coriander
ground turmeric
ground cinnamon and
  cinnamon sticks
sweet paprika
crushed dried chillies/hot
  red pepper flakes

Seasonings and
flavourings
coarse sea salt
black peppercorns
soy sauce (light and dark)
Tabasco
teriyaki sauce
smooth Dijon mustard
runny honey
vanilla extract

Fresh foods
a bag of onions

a head of garlic
2–3 red chillies/chiles
fresh ginger
fresh herbs, such as parsley
carrots
potatoes
tomatoes
lemons, limes, oranges,
  apples and pears

In the refrigerator
eggs
milk
unsalted butter
a wedge of Parmesan
  cheese
feta cheese
Greek yogurt

In the Freezer
vanilla ice cream
frozen peas
ice cubes

Extra items:
Staples
couscous or bulgur wheat
strong white bread flour
easy-blend/active dried
  yeast
jumbo oats
sultanas or raisins

cocoa powder
(caster) sugar
muscovado/brown sugar

Oils and vinegars
small bottles of sesame oil
  and walnut oil

Spices
saffron threads

Seasonings and
flavourings
Thai fish sauce
horseradish sauce
tomato chutney
wholegrain Dijon mustard
English mustard powder
sun-dried tomatoes and
  peppers
black olives
capers
red wine
brandy
Marsala or sherry

Fresh foods
your choice of other herbs,
  such as chives, basil, thyme
  and rosemary

menu planning

For every day, when there's just you, cook whatever you fancy and serve it however you wish. However, if you're entertaining, menu planning isn't hard – there are just a few basic principles to keep in mind.

number of courses

• Decide on the number of courses – three is common (first/appetizer, main/entrée and dessert). Two is fine also (a main/entrée and something else).

• However, you can add extras – before-dinner snacks, salads, cheese and chocolates after!

• Serving cheese. The French do it before the dessert, the English after, and the Americans serve it any time. Please yourself! Just an idea – if you serve cheese after the main/entrée, you can drink the same wine you had with that.

• Serving salads. Mostly, salad is served after the main/entrée, as a palate cleanser. But you can also have it with the cheese (cheese and leaves are great together) or as a very healthy first course. You can even make an especially big one and have it as the only course for lunch.

balance

• Serve only one cheesy dish in a meal – if you had goat cheese salad for first course, don't serve cheese later.

• If you had a cream sauce with the main/entrée, don't serve cream or ice cream with the pudding.

• If you had pastry or eggs in your first course, don't have them for a main/entrée or pudding.

• If you had seafood for first course, don't have fish for main/entrée – unless of course you have a serious passion for oceanic eating!

• Don't make every course a hot one. People like the contrast of something chilled – and it makes life easier for you, the cook.

colour and texture

• Don't have three courses of pale food. If you have chicken, don't have potato and leek soup. For main/entrée, make sure only one vegetable is white – if you are serving potatoes, for example, avoid serving cauliflower at the same time.

• People like contrasting textures. So if you're having mashed potatoes, don't have another mashed or puréed vegetable. Make the others crunchy.

• But don't make everything crunchy either.

presentation

• Keep it simple.

• When adding a garnish, only add something that's relevant to the dish, and make sure it is edible. So if you've used parsley in the dish for flavouring, garnish with parsley.

• Don't put too much on the plate at once. Think of the rim around the plate as the frame of a picture, and only put food inside the frame.

making life easy

• Make sure at least one course can be prepared a day ahead or in the morning. Braises, tarts (savoury or sweet) and ice cream can all be prepared ahead.

• Make sure you've got room – in the kitchen, in your oven, in the refrigerator, even on the table. Wash up as much as you can before you serve the meal, clear away all the ingredients as you use them to leave room for you to work. It all helps to make life easy.

• Don't ask too many people, or you make life difficult for yourself.

allergies

• When you ask people to dinner, ask them if there's anything they can't eat. They may be allergic, or have religious taboos. Common allergies include wheat, dairy, shellfish, crustacea, fish and nuts. They may be vegetarians – and if they're vegans, they won't be able to eat eggs or dairy foods either.

drinks

• Serve your favourite wines, and don't worry about rules like white wine with white meat and red with red meat.

• Tastes vary, but reckon on about three-quarters of a bottle per person, and ask your friends to bring a bottle.

• With Asian food, I suggest beer or Gewürztraminer wine.

• Always have lots of mineral water, still and sparkling.

tips and techniques

seeding tomatoes

Halve the tomatoes crossways. Squeeze one half gently in one hand. Using the fingertips of your other hand, scrape out the seeds and pulp. Repeat with the remaining half.

lemon and lime juice

To get maximum juice from lemons or limes, roll them up and down on a board with the palm of your hand, pressing down as you roll, before squeezing them.

toasting nuts and seeds

Heat a dry frying pan over a high heat, then add the nuts or seeds in a single layer. Cook for about 1 minute, turning often with a spoon, shaking the pan lightly to move them around, until toasted. Remove the pan from the heat and tip the seeds or nuts onto a cold plate – don't leave them in the pan, or they will carry on toasting until they burn. When toasting larger nuts, spread them out on a baking sheet and cook in a hot oven. Toast for about 5–6 minutes until golden.

chopping herbs

Don't over-chop herbs, or they lose much of their flavour and fragrance. Using kitchen scissors or a very sharp knife, give them just a few chops.

making parmesan cheese shavings

Take a wedge of fresh Parmesan and, using a swivel potato peeler, pull lightly down the side of the cheese towards you to make curls.

cooking dried beans

Personally, I always use canned beans, but if you would like to use dried ones, soak them overnight in cold water to cover, then drain, put in a saucepan, bring to the boil and simmer until tender (up to 2 hours, depending on the age of the beans). Never add salt at the beginning of cooking, or the beans will be tough. Add them 10 minutes before the end.

check the use-by dates

Clear out your cupboards regularly. Check use-by dates and throw away anything you know you won't use. Herbs and spices go stale and lose flavour, so buy small quantities and replace them often. Keep in a cool, dark place out of direct sunlight.

safety notes

Be conscious of food safety – food poisoning can be serious.

• Try to keep dish towels for drying clean dishes only, and use kitchen paper/paper towels for food preparation. If you wipe your hands on a dish towel after handling meat, possible infections can easily spread.

• If cooking previously frozen food, defrost it properly before heating.

• Keep uncooked food refrigerated until you need it – don't leave it hanging around in the kitchen or garden in warm weather.

• Be patient. Never serve sausages, pork, chicken or turkey before they are completely cooked.

• Never put cooked food onto a plate that has had raw meat, poultry or fish on it.

the basics

First things first. Use these chapters to become familiar with all the different methods of cooking. Read the introductory tips in each section and try out the recipes, following the steps to master the techniques.

boiling

Cooking food in a saucepan of boiling water is simple and easy. Just think of all the familiar things you can cook in this way; boiled eggs, pasta and noodles, rice, potatoes and vegetables. It's a fat-free cooking method that preserves the green colour of vegetables and keeps the grains of rice and strands of pasta separate.

boiling tips

- Always fill the saucepan with lots of water – enough to cover the food completely – then bring it to the boil.
- Start with cold water for "old" potatoes, chickpeas, beans and lentils, and boiling water for new potatoes, vegetables, noodles, pasta and rice.
- Lid on or off? Keep the lid off for long grain rice, pasta, noodles, green vegetables and new potatoes – put the lid on for other kinds of rice, "old" potatoes and other root vegetables.
- If the lid is on, keep it slightly ajar, or the pan will boil over.
- For variations on boiling, see Poaching (page 24) and Braising (page 86).

blanching, refreshing and par-boiling

- Blanching means partially cooking foods, especially vegetables, by dunking them briefly in boiling water. This is especially good for green beans and broccoli, when you want a good, crunchy salad or if you are going to stir-fry the vegetables afterwards. Drain as soon as they turn a bright green, then refresh (see below).
- Refreshing is when the blanched food is plunged into iced water to stop it cooking and to set the colour. Drain again when it's cold.
- Par-boiling is when the foods, often vegetables, are half cooked by boiling in order to be finished by some other cooking method, often roasting. Par-boiling potatoes and parsnips before roasting them stops them drying out or shrivelling before they are roasted and cooked through.

classic creamy mashed potatoes

Choose large "old" potatoes – the sort that become fluffy when mashed. Buy a good potato peeler – the kind with a swivel blade. These are simple, old-fashioned utensils and, for some reason, they become sharper with age. When boiling potatoes, it's always important to add salt before cooking.

1 kg/2 lbs. large "old" potatoes, such as baking potatoes, peeled and cut into 5-cm/2-inch cubes
about 150 ml/⅔ cup milk, preferably hot
40 g/3 tablespoons butter
salt and freshly ground black pepper

serves 4

1 Put the potatoes in a medium saucepan. Add cold water to cover and a pinch of salt.

2 Bring to the boil, reduce the heat, cover with a lid and simmer for 15–20 minutes until tender when pierced with a knife. Drain and return the potatoes to the pan.

3 Return the saucepan to the heat and mash the potatoes with a fork or potato masher for 30 seconds – this will steam off any excess water.

4 Stir in the milk and butter with a spoon.

5 Mash until smooth, adding extra milk if needed and salt and pepper to taste. Serve immediately, in a serving bowl or straight onto dinner plates.

crushed herb mash

In this recipe, the potatoes are lightly crushed rather than mashed – they shouldn't be smooth. The garlic is cooked in the potato water until very soft, then crushed with the potatoes.

750 g/1½ lbs. large "old" potatoes, cut into
    2.5-cm/1-inch cubes
4 garlic cloves, peeled
4 tablespoons extra virgin olive oil
½ teaspoon grated lemon zest
a bunch of basil, leaves torn
salt and freshly ground black pepper

serves 4

Put the potatoes and garlic into a saucepan, add a pinch of salt and cover with cold water. Bring to the boil, reduce the heat, cover with a lid and simmer for about 12 minutes until tender when pierced with a knife.

When the potatoes are nearly cooked, put the oil in a small saucepan, add the lemon zest and heat gently for 1 minute. Add the basil and heat for a further 20–30 seconds until it turns bright green.

Drain the potatoes and garlic and return them to the pan. Add the infused oil and salt and pepper to taste. Using a potato masher or fork, gently crush the potatoes, garlic and oil. Serve immediately.

classic creamy mashed potatoes

MASHED POTATO TIPS

• Best for mashing are large "old" potatoes (often called floury or baking potatoes). They become light and fluffy when boiled.

• Cut them into evenly sized pieces, so they will cook at the same rate and all be ready at the same time.

• Always start the potatoes in COLD water. Bring to the boil, then simmer – with the lid slightly ajar – until tender when pierced with the point of a knife.

• Never use a food processor to mash your potatoes – you'll end up with wallpaper glue!

flavoured mashed potatoes

Add extra flavourings to the basic mashed potato recipe opposite:

mustard mash Add 2 tablespoons English mustard and 3 tablespoons chopped parsley at the same time as the milk and butter.

sun-dried tomato mash Add 2 tablespoons sun-dried tomato paste, 50 g/⅔ cup freshly grated Parmesan cheese and 3 tablespoons chopped basil at the same time as the milk and butter.

horseradish mash Add 3–4 tablespoons creamed horseradish sauce at the same time as the milk and butter. Serve sprinkled with chopped dill.

spring vegetable vinaigrette

The vegetables in this recipe are blanched and refreshed in iced water (page 15) to bring out their lovely bright colour and snappy texture. Have the bowl of iced water ready and, as soon as the vegetables are blanched, transfer them straight into the iced water. I think of this dish as a real celebration of spring, so prefer to use fresh peas, but if you can't find them, frozen will do instead.

4–6 asparagus spears
125 g/1 cup mangetout/snowpeas
125 g/1 cup sugar snap peas
125 g/1 cup shelled fresh peas
3 tablespoons olive oil
1 garlic clove, thickly sliced
salt and freshly ground black pepper
1 lemon, cut into wedges, to serve

serves 4

Using a small, sharp knife, trim off about 1 cm/½ inch from the stalk end of the asparagus spears. Cut the trimmed spears in half lengthways.

Bring a large saucepan of water to the boil. Meanwhile, fill a large bowl with ice and cold water, so that it is ready to refresh the vegetables as soon as they are cooked. Add the asparagus, mangetout/snowpeas and sugar snap peas to the boiling water. Cover and return to the boil, then remove the lid and add the peas. Boil for a further 30 seconds.

Drain the vegetables, then tip them into the iced water to refresh.

Meanwhile, put the oil and garlic in a small saucepan and heat gently for 1 minute, to infuse. Remove the garlic and discard.

Drain the vegetables well, then spread sheets of kitchen paper/paper towel on a work surface. Put the vegetables on top and let them dry off a little. Transfer them to a large serving plate and pour over the infused oil. Sprinkle with plenty of salt and pepper and serve with lemon wedges.

BOILING GREEN VEGETABLES

• Plunge them into a saucepan of BOILING water (never cold).

• Boil them with the lid off – this preserves some of the nutrients and bright colour and stops them from going soggy.

• Refresh in iced water as described on page 15, if using in cold dishes. If serving hot, serve straightaway.

new potato salad with gazpacho dressing

Gazpacho is the famous Spanish chilled soup, made with tomatoes, (bell) peppers, onions and garlic. Use the same ingredients to make a fresh dressing for this simple salad of new potatoes. Add the dressing to the potatoes while they are hot, even if you aren't eating them straightaway, as this will help the flavours to infuse.

500 g/1 lb. baby new potatoes, scrubbed but not peeled

GAZPACHO DRESSING
2 large, ripe tomatoes, halved, seeded (page 11) and diced
50 g/2 oz. preserved roasted red peppers (in a jar), diced
½ small red onion, chopped
1 garlic clove, chopped
3 tablespoons extra virgin olive oil
2 teaspoons red wine vinegar
a pinch of sugar
a bunch of flat leaf parsley, coarsely chopped
salt and freshly ground black pepper

serves 4

Bring a large saucepan of water to the boil, add the potatoes and return to the boil. Reduce the heat and simmer for about 12 minutes or until the potatoes are just tender when pierced with a knife.

Meanwhile, put the dressing ingredients into a large bowl and mix well. Add plenty of salt and freshly ground pepper.

Drain the potatoes thoroughly and tip them into the dressing. Mix well and serve hot or let cool to room temperature.

COOKING NEW POTATOES

• New potatoes are firm and waxy, perfect for salads, or for serving whole, tossed in butter.

• Cook them unpeeled, or rub off their thin skins with a cloth.

• Plunge them into a saucepan of boiling water (never cold) and simmer, with the lid off, until done.

new potato salad with gazpacho dressing

simple spaghetti with capers and olives

Don't be tempted to add oil to the pasta cooking water – it is a myth that it stops pasta sticking and is a waste of good oil! Just stir occasionally with a wooden spoon while it is cooking.

375 g/13 oz. dried spaghetti
6 tablespoons virgin olive oil
2 garlic cloves, finely chopped
2 tablespoons capers, drained and rinsed,
    plus a few caperberries (optional)
12 kalamata olives, pitted and coarsely chopped
freshly squeezed juice of ½ lemon
8 tablespoons coarsely chopped flat leaf parsley
salt and freshly ground black pepper
fresh Parmesan cheese shavings (page 11), to serve (optional)

serves 4

Cook the spaghetti in a large saucepan of boiling, salted water, as directed on the packet, until cooked, or "al dente".

While the spaghetti is cooking, gently heat the oil in a small saucepan. Add the garlic and cook for 1 minute. Add the capers, olives and lemon juice and cook for a 30 seconds. When the pasta is cooked, drain and return it to the warm pan. Add the caper mixture and parsley and toss well

to coat. Add freshly ground black pepper and Parmesan shavings, if using, and serve.

penne with cheese, prosciutto and spinach

Drain penne really well, because the water gets caught in the tubes.

375 g/13 oz. dried penne
2 egg yolks
125 g/½ cup mascarpone cheese
50 g/⅔ cup Parmesan cheese, freshly grated
50 g/1 cup baby spinach leaves
a handful of wild rocket/arugula
½ tablespoon extra virgin olive oil
8 slices prosciutto, each torn into 3 pieces
salt and freshly ground black pepper

serves 4

Cook the penne in a large saucepan of boiling, salted water, as directed on the package, until cooked, or "al dente".

While the pasta is cooking, put the egg yolks, mascarpone and Parmesan in a bowl and mix well. Add plenty of black pepper.

Put the spinach, rocket/arugula and oil into a large bowl. Toss well, adding black pepper to taste.

When the pasta is cooked, drain and return it to the warm pan. Put the pan over a low heat and add the mascarpone mixture. Stir for about 30 seconds to mix. Divide the pasta between 4 pasta bowls, top each with a handful of rocket/arugula and spinach and finish with the prosciutto.

simple spaghetti with capers and olives

BOILING PASTA

• Bring a large saucepan of water to the boil, then add the pasta.

• Boil with the lid off and keep it boiling until the pasta is cooked.

• To test whether it's cooked, remove a piece with tongs, then bite it. It should be soft, but still slightly firm to the bite. This is called "al dente", which literally means "to the tooth" in Italian.

• Follow package directions and taste often.

warm thai crab rice noodles

chillied chive egg noodles

Egg noodles are made with egg and wheat flour, and there are thick and thin kinds. They take longer to cook than rice noodles (made from rice flour) or beanthread/cellophane noodles (made from mung bean flour).

250 g/8 oz. dried egg noodles
50 g/4 tablespoons butter
2 tablespoons chilli oil
a large bunch of chives, coarsely chopped
juice of ½ lemon
salt and freshly ground black pepper

serves 8 as an accompaniment

Cook the noodles in a saucepan of boiling water until tender, 5 minutes, or as directed on the package. Drain, rinse in cold water and set aside.

Heat the butter and oil in a large saucepan or wok until hot. Add the noodles and toss until heated through. Add the chives and lemon juice and toss well to coat. Add salt and pepper to taste and serve at once.

warm thai crab rice noodles

Rice noodles cook very quickly, so be careful not to overcook them. Rinsing them in boiling water removes excess starch and keeps them in strands, not clumps.

250 g/8 oz. dried rice noodles, preferably thin
340 g/12 oz. canned white crabmeat, drained, or 200 g/7 oz. fresh

DRESSING
2 tablespoons sunflower/safflower oil
1 medium red chilli, finely chopped
1 medium green chilli, finely chopped
2.5-cm/1-inch piece of fresh ginger, peeled and finely chopped
grated zest of 1 lime and juice of 2 limes
1 tablespoon Thai fish sauce
leaves from a large bunch of coriander/cilantro
50 g/⅓ cup cashew nuts, lightly toasted (page 11)
salt and freshly ground black pepper

serves 4 as starter/appetizer, light lunch or dinner

Soak or cook noodles as directed on the package. Meanwhile, boil the kettle and put the crabmeat into a large bowl.

To make the dressing, put the oil in another bowl. Add the chillies, ginger, lime zest and juice, fish sauce and coriander/cilantro. Stir, then add to the bowl of crabmeat. Add salt and pepper to taste.

When the noodles are cooked, drain and rinse with the kettle of boiling water. Return the noodles to their bowl or pan, then add half the crab mixture and half the cashew nuts. Toss well.

Divide the noodles between 4 plates and top each with a spoonful of the remaining crab mixture. Sprinkle with the remaining nuts and serve.

BOILING NOODLES

• Cook noodles in the same way as pasta, but don't add salt to the cooking water, because this will mask their flavour.

• Add salt AFTER cooking. If adding soy sauce or fish sauce – the salts of Asia – you won't need to add salt as well.

• Rinse cooked rice noodles in boiling water to stop them from sticking together.

cardamom and orange buttered rice

Start testing a few grains of rice before it should be done, and keep checking as it cooks – that way, you won't overcook it.

10 cardamom pods
375 g/2 cups long grain rice
2 fresh bay leaves
a large strip of orange zest
25 g/2 tablespoons butter
salt and freshly ground black pepper

serves 4

Split open the cardamom pods, discard the shells, and lightly crush the seeds with a mortar and pestle. Alternatively, put the seeds on a board and use the back of a spoon to crush them lightly.

Bring a large saucepan of water to the boil. Add the rice, bay leaves, orange zest and cardamom seeds. Return to the boil, reduce the heat to a simmer and cook with the lid off for about 12 minutes until the rice is just cooked. Drain well through a sieve/strainer.

Return the pan to the heat and add the butter. When melted, add the rice, stir well, add salt and pepper to taste and serve.

---

smoky puy lentils with balsamic vinegar and pancetta

Chickpeas and beans need presoaking before boiling. However, lentils do not, so this is a quick and easy dish. Do keep an eye on them as they cook as they can dry out quickly and may need extra boiling water added.

5 red (bell) peppers, quartered lengthways and seeded
3 large red onions, cut into 8 wedges each
8 tablespoons olive oil
500 g/2¼ cups Puy or brown lentils, rinsed
3 tablespoons balsamic vinegar
6 unpeeled garlic cloves
125 g/4 oz. pancetta or (streaky) bacon, diced
salt and freshly ground black pepper

serves 4

Preheat the oven to 200°C (400°F) Gas 6.

Put the (bell) peppers and onions into a large roasting pan. Pour over 3 tablespoons of the oil and add plenty of salt and pepper. Roast in the preheated oven for 30 minutes.

Meanwhile, to cook the lentils, put them into a large saucepan and add 1 litre/4 cups (twice their volume) of cold water. Bring to the boil, remove the lid and cook at a fast simmer until the water has been absorbed and the lentils are tender, about 20–25 minutes.

Put the remaining oil and balsamic vinegar into a small bowl and whisk well. Add the garlic and pancetta or bacon to the onions and (bell) peppers and roast for 15 minutes more or until golden. Remove from the oven.

Squeeze the insides of the roasted garlic out of their skins into the balsamic dressing and mix. Drain the cooked lentils and put them into a large bowl. Pour in the dressing, add salt and pepper to taste and stir through.

Add half the roasted vegetables and pancetta to the lentils, stir gently, then transfer to a serving dish. Spoon the remaining vegetables and pancetta or bacon on top and serve.

BOILING RICE

• Cook long grain rice in a large saucepan and plenty of boiling water, until tender but still with a slight bite in the middle, about 12–15 minutes, with the lid off.

• To cook basmati and Thai fragrant rice, rinse to remove the starch, put in a large saucepan and add cold water to 2.5 cm/1 inch above the rice level. Cover with a lid and bring to the boil, reduce the heat and simmer until the water is absorbed, about 5 minutes. Remove the pan from the heat and let stand, with the lid on, for about 10 minutes until cooked.

smoky puy lentils with balsamic
vinegar and pancetta

thai fish broth

poaching

Poaching is a gentle way of cooking and is a variation of boiling. The cooking liquid is brought to the boil, then the heat is reduced so the liquid is barely trembling, with few bubbles breaking the surface. It is a good way of cooking delicate foods, such as fish or eggs, which break up when boiled – or chicken, which becomes tough when boiled. In China and South-east Asia, poaching is done in a wok.

poaching tips

- Poach in simmering, not boiling, liquid. It should be barely trembling when the food goes in.
- To get to simmering, boil the liquid in a saucepan or wok with the lid on. Remove the lid, reduce the heat and wait for the bubbles to subside.
- Add the food carefully to the liquid and always poach with the lid off, to let the steam escape.
- Use a slotted spoon to remove food from its poaching liquid. If you are keeping the liquid, for example if it is stock, drain through a sieve/strainer or colander into a bowl.

liquids for poaching

- You can poach in any liquid – water, stock (chicken, fish or vegetable), milk or coconut milk.
- Water is the most basic poaching medium – as it is flavourless, you need to season it well before adding the food.
- Chicken or vegetable stock is good for poaching chicken, which will have a richer flavour. In Asian cooking, fish, also, is often cooked in chicken stock.
- Milk: bring it almost to the boil – take care because it boils over easily. This is good for poaching fish, especially smoked fish.
- Coconut milk: bring it almost to the boil – if it boils it will curdle. This is used for Asian dishes.

poaching eggs

- Poaching is a classic way to cook eggs.

To poach an egg, bring a deep saucepan of lightly salted water to the boil. Add 1 tablespoon white wine vinegar and reduce the heat to a simmer. Crack the egg into a cup and swirl the water with a fork to create a whirlpool effect. Slide the egg into the water. Cook for 3 minutes, then remove with a slotted spoon. Sit the spoon on a piece of kitchen paper on a plate, let drain for 10 seconds, then serve.

thai fish broth

thai fish broth

Thai curries often use the poaching method. It is a good way to cook the delicate flesh of fish and seafood and the poaching liquid becomes the sauce or broth. Thai curry pastes are easy to make, but you can also buy them. Pastes vary in heat, so taste first – you'll need 2–3 tablespoons.

about 600 ml/2¾ cups vegetable stock

400 g/14 oz. canned coconut milk

375 g/12 oz. salmon fillet, cut into chunks

250 g/8 oz. uncooked tiger prawns/jumbo shrimp,
    peeled but with the tails on

125 g/1 cup sugar snap peas, halved lengthways

2 tablespoons basil leaves, torn

freshly squeezed juice of 1 lime

freshly ground black pepper

cooked Thai fragrant rice (page 22), to serve

THAI CURRY PASTE

1 tablespoon oil

4–5 tablespoons of the coconut milk

5 cm/2 inches fresh ginger, peeled and chopped

1 green chilli, halved, seeded and chopped (page 43)

1 red chilli, halved, seeded and chopped (page 43)

1 tablespoon chopped lemongrass

1 teaspoon coriander seeds

1 shallot, chopped

1 garlic clove, chopped

1 teaspoon salt

serves 4

1 To make the Thai curry paste, put all the paste ingredients into a blender or food processor and blend briefly.

2 The texture should be a coarse paste.

3 Heat a wok over medium heat, add the paste and stir-fry for 2 minutes. This will release the flavours of the spices. ⇨

POACHING IN COCONUT MILK

• If coconut milk boils, it "splits" (curdles).

• Bring it to just below boiling, then reduce the heat until barely simmering.

• Canned coconut cream won't curdle, so use it if available.

• Don't worry too much if it does curdle (Asian cooks don't).

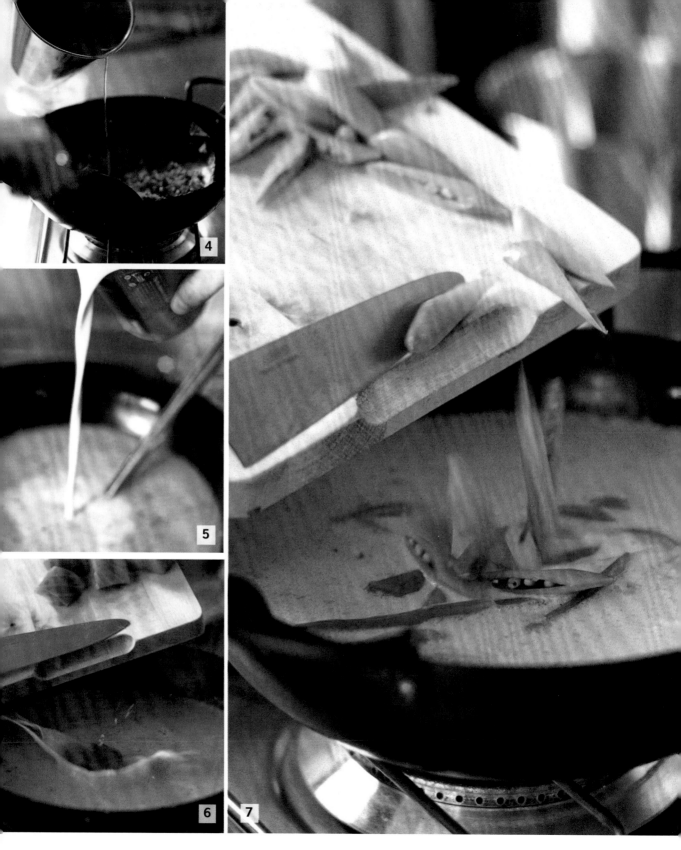

8

4 Add the stock.

5 Add the coconut milk and heat to simmering, so that the liquid is just moving.

6 Add the salmon and prawns/shrimp. Bring back to simmering, then cook for 2 minutes.

7 Add the sugar snap peas. Cook for a further 1 minute until the fish is just cooked (it will be opaque all the way through).

8 Add half the basil leaves and salt and pepper to taste, then stir. Add the lime juice and sprinkle with the remaining basil leaves. Spoon a share of rice into each bowl, ladle the broth over the top, then serve.

wholegrain mustard tarragon chicken

Chicken is excellent poached in stock – the result is rich but healthy. Keep the leftover stock in this recipe to use another time.

4 large sprigs of tarragon
2 litres/8 cups chicken or vegetable stock
4 boneless, skinless chicken breasts
125 g/1 cup salad leaves
crusty bread, to serve

MUSTARD DRESSING
4 tablespoons extra virgin olive oil
1 teaspoon wholegrain mustard
salt and freshly ground black pepper

serves 4

Strip the tarragon leaves from the stalks, reserve the leaves and put the stalks and the stock into a large saucepan. Cover with a lid and bring to the boil, then remove the lid and reduce the heat to a very gentle simmer, so the stock is barely moving.

Put the chicken breasts between 2 pieces of clingfilm/plastic wrap and, using a rolling pin, bash and flatten each piece to 1 cm/½ inch thickness. Remove and discard the clingfilm/plastic wrap.

Put the flattened chicken pieces into the stock and poach gently for about 12–15 minutes until firm to the touch and cooked through, with no trace of pink in the middle. Drain and let cool a little, reserving the stock for another recipe. (Keep refrigerated for up to 3 days or freeze it.)

Meanwhile, coarsely chop the tarragon leaves and put in a mini-blender. Add the dressing ingredients and 1 teaspoon water and blend for 1–2 minutes until smooth.

Slice the chicken diagonally into finger-size strips. Divide the salad leaves between 4 large plates and top with the slices of chicken. Drizzle with the dressing and serve immediately with crusty bread.

POACHING IN STOCK

• Poaching in stock will add flavour to the food being cooked in it.

• You can use chicken or vegetable stock for chicken, but you don't have to use fish stock for fish – you can also use chicken stock, vegetable stock or milk.

steamed sweet baby carrots
with orange

steaming

Steamed food is cooked by trapped vapour from heated liquid. An indirect form of heat, it may be created in a saucepan, in a foil package, or by a tray of water in the oven. The food is cooked by moist heat and retains all its juices and flavours. If you like fat-free cooking, this is one of the methods for you.

pan-steaming

- Set a perforated steamer over simmering water in a saucepan, wok or frying pan.
- Half-fill the pan or wok with water – there should be enough not to boil dry, but it should not reach the food, or it will boil, not steam.
- Add the food to the steamer only once the water has come to the boil, then cover the pan with a lid to trap the steam.
- To steam fish, line the perforations with a cloth (muslin/cheesecloth) to stop it sticking or breaking up.

Steamers available include:

- A collapsible perforated plate on little legs (see left) which can be put into any saucepan or pan, and the food arranged on top.
- A metal saucepan-steamer set, with a steamer like a second saucepan with holes in the bottom.
- Chinese bamboo steamers.
- Other utensils can also be used – try a colander or metal sieve/strainer set over a pan of boiling water.

foil-steaming

- Cut out a square of foil, put the food in the middle, fold so the foil overlaps on top, then scrunch the edges of foil together to seal.
- Cook in a steamer, in the oven or on a barbecue/grill. The food will be cooked by the steam trapped inside the foil.

oven-steaming

- Put small ovenproof dishes in a deep roasting pan.
- Pour boiling water to reach halfway up the sides of the dishes, then cover the whole pan tightly with foil, to trap the steam.
- Put the pan in a preheated oven to cook.

steamed sweet baby carrots with orange

This is the simplest form of steaming and a good way to cook many vegetables, such as broccoli, cauliflower and beans. They cook to perfection in the steamy heat – healthy and delicious! If you don't have a special steamer, use a colander or sieve/strainer set over a pan of boiling water instead.

500 g/1 lb. baby carrots, halved lengthways
a strip of orange peel
freshly squeezed juice of 2 oranges
15 g/1 tablespoon butter
1 teaspoon sugar
a pinch of salt
2 tablespoons coarsely chopped coriander/cilantro leaves
freshly ground black pepper

serves 4

Put about 2 cm/¾ inch water in a large saucepan. Cover and bring to the boil over a high heat. Put the carrots into a metal or bamboo steamer or colander and put into or over the pan. Reduce the heat and simmer for 5–8 minutes, or until the carrots are just tender.

Meanwhile, put the orange peel, juice, butter, sugar and salt into a small saucepan. Heat until boiling, then reduce the heat and simmer gently for about 5 minutes until reduced by half. Remove and discard the orange peel.

Put the steamed carrots into a serving dish. Add the coriander/cilantro and orange mixture and toss well. Add plenty of black pepper and serve.

STEAMING FISH IN A WOK

• Method 1: Cover the bottom of a wok with water, add a plate, upside down, so it doesn't touch the water. Put the fish on top, cover with the wok lid and heat until steaming.
• Method 2: Put a plate in a bamboo steamer, add the fish and flavourings, then steam in the usual way. The fish won't break up, and the flavourings will seep into the flesh.

---

steamed mussels with garlic and vermouth in a foil package

When you make a package of foil, the vermouth turns to steam and cooks the mussels in a delicious scented vapour. Let everyone open their own package – as they open it up, the scented steam smells heavenly.

1 kg/2 lbs. mussels, in their shells
50 g/3 tablespoons butter
150 ml/⅔ cup dry vermouth
2 garlic cloves, crushed

TO SERVE
crusty bread
a bunch of flat leaf parsley, coarsely chopped (optional)
4 pieces of foil, about 60 x 30 cm/24 x 12 inches
1 baking sheet

serves 4

Preheat the oven to 200°C (400°F) Gas 6.

Scrub the mussels clean and rinse them in several changes of cold water to remove grit. Pull off the beards or seaweed-like threads and discard any mussels that are cracked or that don't close when tapped against the kitchen counter – these are dead and not edible.

Fold each piece of foil in half lengthways and divide the butter, vermouth, garlic and mussels between them. Bring the corners of each piece together to close each package, leaving a little space in each one so the mussels with have room to open. Pinch the edges of the packages together to seal.

Put the packages on a baking sheet and transfer to the preheated oven. Cook for 10–12 minutes or until all the mussels have opened – check by opening one of the packages (being careful as the steam will be very hot).

Put the packages on heated plates and serve with crusty bread to mop up the delicious juices.

If you like, put coarsely chopped parsley in a bowl and serve separately for people to sprinkle over their mussels when they open the packages.

steamed mussels with garlic and
vermouth in a foil package

lime and ginger honey puddings

Putting dishes in a tray of hot water creates a bain-marie. It produces a gentler heat than direct oven heat, and makes for lighter results.

2 tablespoons (runny) honey
3 pieces stem ginger, finely chopped
1 tablespoon stem ginger syrup
grated zest and juice of 2 limes
85 g/6 tablespoons butter, softened (room temperature)
85 g/⅓ cup (caster) sugar
2 eggs, beaten
85 g/½ cup self-raising flour
double/heavy cream or vanilla ice cream, to serve
4 ramekin dishes, buttered

serves 4

Preheat the oven to 200°C (400°F) Gas 6.

1 Put the honey, ginger and syrup into a bowl, add the juice of 1½ limes and mix well.

2 Put the ramekins in a roasting pan and divide the mixture equally between them.

3 Put the butter and sugar into a bowl and whisk until light and fluffy. Gradually add the beaten eggs, whisking all the time.

4 Sift the flour into the mixture, add the lime zest and remaining lime juice and fold in (mix gently) with a large metal spoon.

5 Spoon on top of the honey and ginger mixture, dividing the mixture equally between the ramekins.

6 Pour enough boiling water into the pan to come halfway up the sides of the ramekins.

7 Cover the whole roasting pan with foil and seal tightly around the edges.

8 Transfer to the preheated oven and cook for about 40 minutes until soft and springy on top and a skewer inserted in the middle comes out clean.

Run a knife round the edges to loosen, turn out onto plates and serve hot with cream or ice cream.

COOKING IN A STEAM BATH

• Cooking food in dishes set in a roasting pan of hot water is a very gentle way of cooking. It is often used for egg dishes, so the eggs won't overheat and curdle.

• The steam bath is called a bain-marie.

microwaving

Microwaves use intense heat created by high-speed waves to cook food very quickly. They are good for cooking green vegetables, fish and steamed puddings. It's a handy stand-by, but should never be considered as an oven in its own right.

microwave tips

- Don't lose the instruction booklet that comes with your microwave. For successful microwave cooking, always follow the manufacturer's instructions to the letter.
- Never put metal in any form into your microwave. This includes roasting pans, foil or crockery with gold or silver leaf. It is dangerous and damages the oven.
- Plastic, ovenproof glass, ceramic or special microwave dishes are best.
- If using clingfilm/plastic wrap, buy special microwave-safe brands. It should be vented at one corner. Don't use with the browning unit – it will melt.
- Cover the food with a lid, plastic or a saucer or plate, but check if the covering should be loose, otherwise the food may boil over and splatter your oven.
- Smaller, evenly sized foods will take less time to cook than one large piece. If cooking "baked" potatoes, they will cook more evenly if you arrange them in a circle.
- Wipe out the oven with a damp cloth every time you use it.

- Don't salt the food before microwaving or it may dry out or become tough.
- Let dishes stand for a few minutes after microwaving to distribute the heat evenly.
- Always check food halfway through cooking time. The heat is very powerful and food may take less time to cook than you think. Some dishes also need stirring halfway through the cooking time.
- See page 39 for information on microwave settings and power levels.

microwave strengths

Microwaves are especially good for:

- Cooking vegetables, such as broccoli and carrots.
- Steaming firm white fish (such as cod) if you are short of time.
- Softening butter.
- Melting chocolate.
- Warming milk.
- Heating up previously cooked dishes. Make sure they are piping hot before serving.

broccoli trees with pan-fried pine nuts

This is about as speedy as it gets! Broccoli is ideal for the microwave, as the stalks and florets cook evenly.

500 g/1 lb. broccoli
25 g/2 tablespoons butter
50 g/½ cup pine nuts
salt and freshly ground black pepper

serves 4

Cut the broccoli into medium florets, leaving a long stalk. Put into a large, microwave-safe bowl, add 50 ml/¼ cup water, cover with microwave-safe clingfilm/plastic wrap or a lid and microwave on HIGH for 3 minutes.

Meanwhile, put the butter, pine nuts and salt and pepper to taste in a small saucepan over medium heat. Cook for 2–3 minutes until the nuts are golden and the butter is foaming.

Drain the broccoli through a colander or sieve/strainer, return to the bowl and toss with the pine nuts and butter. Serve immediately or let cool and serve as a salad.

warm chunky fish pâté

Flake the cooked fish into big pieces – this shouldn't be a smooth pâté.

150 g/6 oz. salmon fillet, skin on

150 ml/⅔ cup white wine

125 g/½ cup cream cheese

4 tablespoons Greek yogurt

2 tablespoons coarsely chopped dill

a squeeze of fresh lemon juice

salt and freshly ground black pepper

TO SERVE

black rye bread, toasted

1 lemon, cut into wedges

serves 4

Put the salmon, skin side up, in a shallow microwave dish. Add the wine and cover with microwave-safe clingfilm/plastic wrap. Cook on MEDIUM for 5 minutes.

Meanwhile, put the cream cheese, yogurt, dill and lemon juice in a large bowl and mix.

Drain the fish on kitchen paper/paper towels and flake into large pieces. Gently fold the fish into the cream cheese mixture and season to taste.

Serve with bread or toast and lemon wedges.

saucy chocolate pots

These gooey pots show how versatile the microwave can be.

100 g/generous ⅓ cup mascarpone or cream cheese

115 g/⅔ cup muscovado/light brown sugar

25 g/¼ cup cocoa powder

2 eggs

1 teaspoon vanilla extract

40 g/¼ cup self-raising flour

thick cream, to serve

4 ramekins, 150 ml/⅔ cup each, buttered

serves 4

Put all the ingredients into a large bowl or food processor. Beat with an electric whisk or process until blended. Divide the mixture among the ramekins.

Cover each ramekin loosely with microwave-safe clingfilm/plastic wrap. Put 2 of the ramekins, spaced well apart, on the microwave tray and cook on HIGH for 1 minute 15 seconds. Let stand with the clingfilm/plastic wrap on while you microwave the remaining 2 pots. As soon as the second 2 pots are cooked, remove the clingfilm/plastic wrap from the first 2. Let the second 2 stand for 2 minutes. Remove the clingfilm/plastic wrap and serve with thick cream.

honey teriyaki vegetables

stir-frying

Stir-fried food is cooked in an open pan or wok over a high heat. It is a healthy, fast way to cook, using only minimal oil. The food is constantly moved around a large surface area of hot pan and cooks evenly and quickly. A wok is absolutely ideal for stir-frying and, of all the pans in my kitchen, it's probably the one that I use the most.

which wok?

- Buy a wok with a lid, so you can also use it for making soups and stews, or steaming (page 30).
- Non-stick woks are ideal and can be used for all sorts of dishes, including big batches of scrambled eggs and super-thin omelettes.
- If you have an electric stove top, choose a wok with a flat bottom.
- If you don't have a wok, a large frying pan can be used instead.

wok cooking tips

- Have all the ingredients prepared and ready – stir-frying is a speedy process, and you won't have time to peel and chop once you start.
- Chop vegetables or meat into evenly sized pieces so that they all cook at the same rate.

- Heat the wok or pan first before adding any oil, to prevent the oil from burning.
- Stir-fry over a high heat – the food must be cooked quickly to be crunchy.
- Don't walk away! Stir the food constantly with a wooden spatula or wok scoop to keep it moving and cooking evenly. Food falls down the sides to the hottest part of the wok in the centre, so keep stirring and flipping the food.
- Don't be tempted to put too much food into the wok or pan at one time, as this reduces the temperature and makes vegetables soggy rather than crunchy.

hot wok chilli shrimp

honey teriyaki vegetables

Teriyaki is a Japanese glaze, made from sake or mirin (rice wines), shoyu (Japanese soy sauce) and sugar. You can buy these ingredients in large supermarkets or Eastern food stores.

2 teaspoons peanut oil
a bunch of radishes, washed, trimmed and halved lengthways
4 carrots, sliced diagonally
a bunch of spring onions/scallions, halved crossways
125 g/1 cup mangetout/snowpeas, halved lengthways
1 tablespoon sesame seeds, toasted (page 11), to serve

DRESSING
1 tablespoon (runny) honey
2 tablespoons teriyaki sauce
freshly ground black pepper

serves 4

To make the dressing, put the honey and teriyaki sauce in a small bowl and mix. Add black pepper to taste.

Put the oil in a wok and heat until hot. Add the vegetables and 2 tablespoons water and stir-fry for about 3 minutes, until the vegetables are just heated through but are still crisp. Transfer to a warm serving dish.

Reduce the heat and return the wok to the heat. Add the dressing and heat it through gently until just warm. Drizzle the dressing over the vegetables, sprinkle with the sesame seeds and serve.

hot wok chilli shrimp

Fast stir-frying is great for seafood, which mustn't be overcooked.

1 red chilli
500 g/1 lb. peeled, uncooked tiger prawns/jumbo shrimp, with the tails on
grated zest and juice of 1 lime
1 garlic clove, chopped
2 tablespoons sunflower/safflower oil
a pinch of sugar

CUCUMBER SALSA
½ cucumber
a bunch of coriander/cilantro
1 tablespoon rice vinegar
1 teaspoon sugar
salt and freshly ground black pepper

serves 4

1 To prepare the chilli, cut it in half lengthways, scrape out the seeds and discard.

2 Cut each half lengthways into fine strips.

3 Cut the strips crossways into very fine dice. ⇨

4 Put the prawns/shrimp into a bowl and add the chilli, lime zest and juice, garlic, 1 tablespoon of the oil and the sugar.

5 Using a potato peeler, remove the peel from the cucumber.

6 Cut the peeled cucumber into slices lengthways, then stack the slices and cut them into strips.

7 Cut the strips crossways into dice.

8 Coarsely chop the coriander/cilantro.

9 Put the cucumber and coriander/cilantro into a second bowl, add the rice vinegar and sugar, then mix, adding salt and pepper to taste.

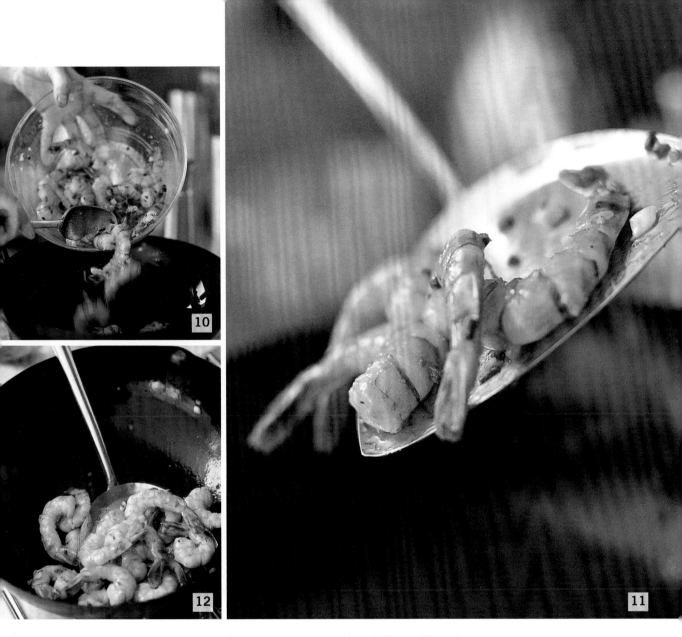

10   Heat the remaining sunflower/safflower oil in a wok over high heat and add half the prawn/shrimp mixture.

11   Stir-fry for 1–2 minutes until pink and cooked. Keep them warm in a very low oven while you stir-fry the remaining prawns/shrimp.

12   When cooked, divide the prawns/shrimp and cucumber salsa between 4 plates and serve.

stir-fried pork in lettuce cups

The pork is stir-fried first, then braised – a typical Chinese cooking method.

500 g/1 lb. minced/ground pork
1 tablespoon peanut oil
1 red (bell) pepper, halved, seeded and finely diced
2 garlic cloves, crushed
a bunch of spring onions/scallions, finely sliced
    with the green tops reserved
3 tablespoons dry sherry
3 tablespoons soy sauce
6 tablespoons oyster sauce
crisp inner leaves from 1 iceberg lettuce, halved
leaves from a bunch of coriander/cilantro
freshly ground black pepper
hoisin sauce, for dipping

serves 4–6

Heat a dry wok until hot, add the pork and cook for 3–4 minutes until opaque. Remove to a plate with a slotted spoon.

Wipe out the wok. Add the oil and heat.

Add the pepper, garlic and spring onions/scallions and cook for 2 minutes. Add the pork and stir-fry for a further minute. Add the sherry and cook for 1 minute.

Stir in the soy and oyster sauces and bring to the boil. Reduce the heat and simmer for 8–10 minutes until the liquid has almost evaporated. Add plenty of black pepper.

Spoon the pork mixture into the lettuce leaf cups and sprinkle with the coriander/cilantro and reserved spring onion/scallion tops. Serve with the hoisin sauce for dipping.

hot chicken tikka platter with yogurt

If you have two woks, use both for this. Otherwise, you can use a large frying pan and a wok.

3 boneless, skinless chicken breasts, cut into strips
juice of 1 lemon
4 tablespoons tikka or mild curry paste
2 garlic cloves, crushed
250 g/8 oz. French beans
1 tablespoon oil
125 g/1 cup baby spinach leaves
freshly ground black pepper

TO SERVE
a bunch of coriander/cilantro, coarsely chopped (optional)
150 g/²⁄₃ cup Greek yogurt

serves 4

Put the chicken strips into a large bowl and sprinkle with the lemon juice. Add the tikka or curry paste and garlic. Mix well. (If time allows, chill and marinate for 30 minutes.)

Heat a large wok or frying pan. Add the chicken with its marinade and cook for 5–7 minutes until the chicken is opaque throughout. Add black pepper to taste.

Meanwhile blanch the beans (page 15) in boiling water. Heat a second wok or large frying pan. Add a tablespoon of oil and, when hot, add the drained beans, remove from the heat and add the spinach leaves. Toss to mix.

To serve, pile the spinach and beans into the centre of a large serving dish. Top with the hot chicken, sprinkle with coriander/cilantro, if using, and serve with Greek yogurt.

hot chicken tikka platter with yogurt

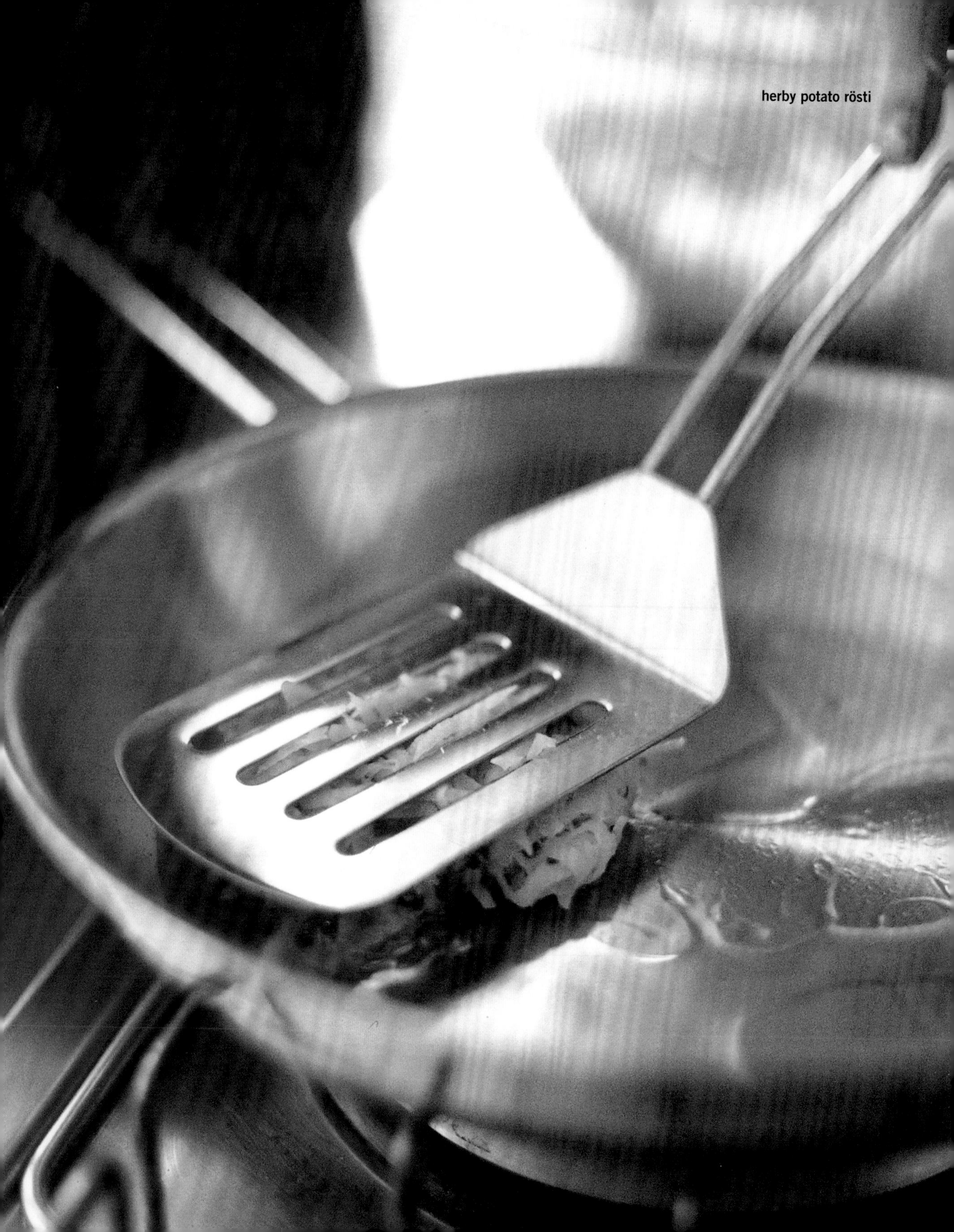

herby potato rösti

frying

Frying is cooking food in an open frying pan with the aid of fat such as butter, oil or a mixture of both. Omelettes, eggs, meats and vegetables are all quickly cooked this way.

frying tips

- Preheat the pan before you add the oil, so that the base of the pan heats evenly.

- Preheat the oil in the pan before adding any food – it should sizzle as it touches the pan. If it's not hot enough, the food will absorb too much oil.

- Don't put a lid on the pan when frying – the food will steam, not fry, and be soggy rather than crisp.

- Don't crowd the pan. Adding too much food at once will lower the temperature of the oil and steam the food. Fry in batches, and keep them warm in the oven while you cook the next batch.

- Put enough oil in the pan for the food to cook evenly on both sides, allowing for some of the fat to be absorbed. This also avoids a tide mark on foods such as fishcakes.

- Don't overheat the oil or heat it for too long. It will break down, start to smoke and taint the flavour.

- Drain fried food on kitchen paper/paper towels and eat it while still hot and crisp.

non-stick pans

- I prefer non-stick pans – buy the best you can afford, the heavier the better.

- Remember, don't overheat the pan, use "kind" utensils, such as wood, be gentle when washing them (don't use scourers) and store hanging up.

choosing oil

- Olive oil is healthier and tastes great (don't fry in extra virgin – save it for salads and finishing foods).

- Peanut and sunflower/safflower oil have little flavour, so use them when you don't want any added taste (for example, when cooking Asian foods).

- When frying in butter, always use unsalted butter, and add a splash of oil to stop it burning (butter burns at a lower temperature than oil).

7

herby potato rösti

Frying creates the lovely crispy crust that's essential for rösti.

3 large potatoes, peeled
3–4 large sage leaves
a sprig of thyme, leaves stripped
4 tablespoons olive oil
salt and freshly ground black pepper

serves 6

1 Grate the potatoes on the coarse side of a box grater and dry well on kitchen paper/paper towels.

2 Finely chop the sage and thyme leaves, discarding any woody stalks.

3 Put the grated potato in a bowl, add the herbs and mix well.

4 Using your hands, shape a big tablespoon of the mixture into a ball.

5 Heat half the oil in a large frying pan until hot. Add the shaped potato cake to the pan and flatten with a long-handled turner or spatula.

6 Shape 2 more potato balls, add to the pan, flatten with the turner and fry for 5 minutes until golden.

7 Turn the rösti over and lower the heat. Continue to cook for 5–10 minutes until golden and cooked through. Transfer to a very low oven to keep them warm. Repeat with the remaining mixture.

Transfer to a serving plate, sprinkle with salt and pepper and serve immediately.

sautéed tomatoes with green pistou

Frying quickly in a very small quantity of oil, as in this recipe, is known as sautéing, from the French word "to jump". I think sautéing is more like stir-frying, but don't toss these tomatoes around too much or they'll break up. Pistou is the French version of pesto – in France it is a herb mix traditionally stirred into soup, but here it is served as a fragrant accompaniment to the crisp-coated tomatoes.

4 large plum tomatoes
50 g/½ cup polenta/cornmeal
½ teaspoon salt
olive oil, for frying
fresh Parmesan cheese shavings (page 11), to serve

PISTOU
3 tablespoons extra virgin olive oil
2 garlic cloves, coarsely chopped
a large bunch of basil
salt and freshly ground black pepper

serves 4

To make the pistou, put the oil, garlic and basil into a small food processor and process until blended. Add salt and pepper to taste.

Cut each tomato crossways into 5 slices and discard the top and bottom slices.

Put the polenta/cornmeal onto a plate, add the salt and mix. Dip the tomato slices into the polenta/cornmeal to coat and transfer to a clean plate.

Put 5 mm/¼ inch oil in a frying pan and heat until hot. Add the tomato slices and fry for 1–2 minutes on each side until the polenta/cornmeal is lightly golden. Remove, drain on kitchen paper/paper towels and sprinkle with salt.

Put 3 tomato slices on each plate, slightly overlapping. Spoon around the pistou, top with the Parmesan shavings, sprinkle with freshly ground black pepper and serve hot.

gremolata pork with lemon spinach

This recipe demonstrates one of the great advantages of shallow-frying. Foods can be coated in breadcrumbs, polenta/ cornmeal, or other crumbly things, then fried gently to give a crisp outside and tender inside.

4 boneless pork chops, 75 g/3 oz. each
1 tablespoon basil oil
50 g/2 oz. ciabatta bread, torn into pieces
4 tablespoons coarsely chopped flat leaf parsley
grated zest of 1 lemon
2 tablespoons olive oil
freshly ground black pepper

LEMON SPINACH
250 g/8 oz. young spinach, washed, dried and finely sliced
1 tablespoon extra virgin olive oil, plus extra for serving
freshly squeezed juice of ½ lemon

serves 4

Trim any excess fat from the pork chops, leaving a thin layer around the meat. Put each chop between 2 pieces of clingfilm/plastic wrap and, using a rolling pin, beat to 5 mm/ ¼ inch thickness.

Remove and discard the clingfilm/plastic wrap and put the pork in a bowl. Add the basil oil and sprinkle with black pepper. Turn to coat, cover and refrigerate for 2 hours.

To make the breadcrumbs, put the ciabatta pieces into a food processor and pulse to coarse crumbs. Put the breadcrumbs, parsley and lemon zest into a bowl and mix. Add black pepper to taste. Transfer to a plate and coat the pork with the crumb mixture, pressing gently until coated on both sides.

Heat the oil in a large frying pan, add the pork and cook for about 2–3 minutes on each side or until the breadcrumbs are golden and the pork is cooked through.

Meanwhile, put the spinach in a large bowl, add the olive oil and lemon juice and toss to coat.

Put a mound of spinach on each plate and top with the pork. Drizzle with the olive oil, sprinkle with freshly ground black pepper and serve.

gremolata pork with lemon spinach

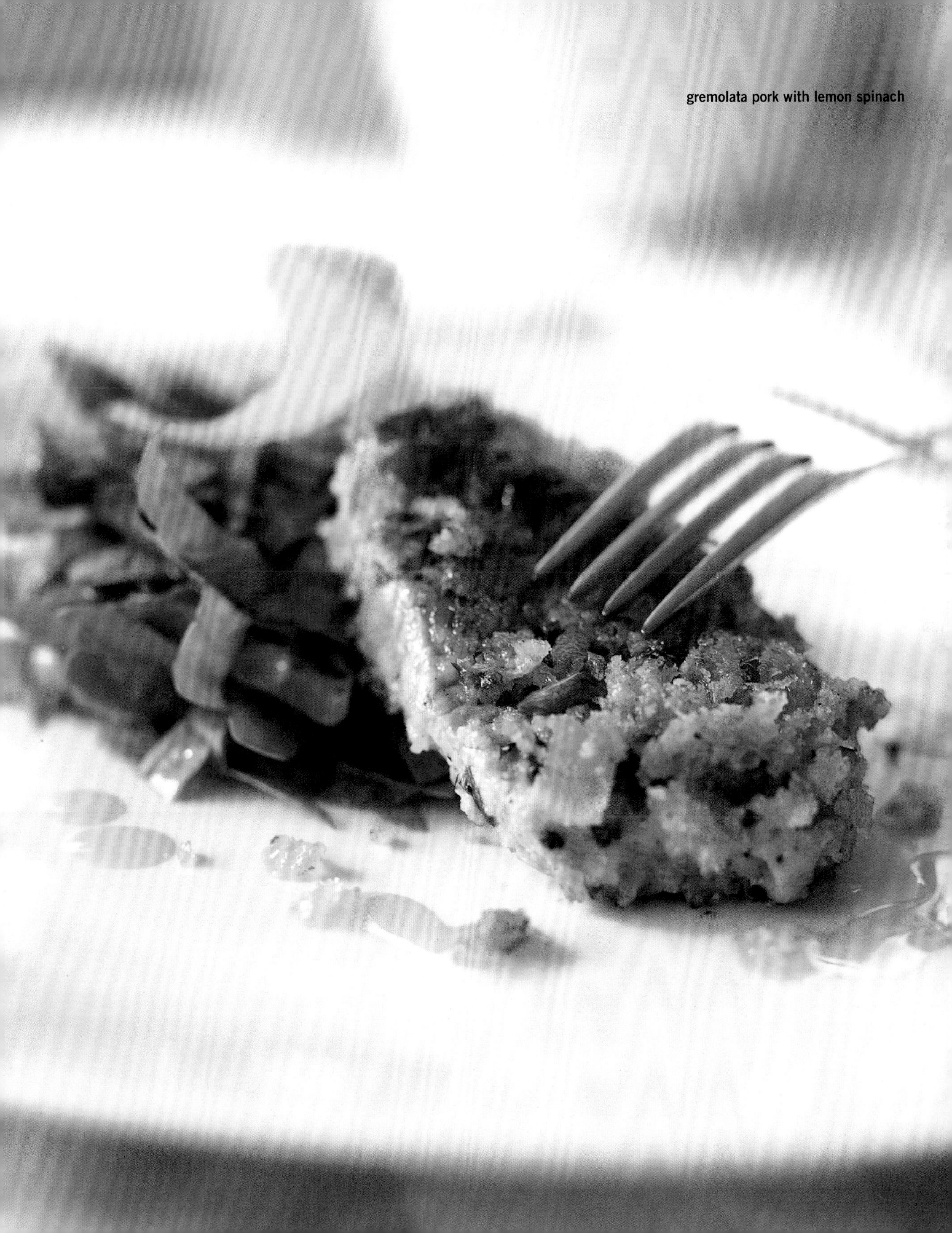

deep-frying

Deep-fried food is cooked by completely immersing in very hot oil. Done properly, it doesn't have to mean greasy fish and soggy fries – deep-fried food, from fries to tempura, should be light and sizzling. Follow these tips for perfect results.

deep-frying tips

- Deep-fry in a large saucepan, deep fryer or wok.
- Do not fill the pan more than half full with oil.
- Use either sunflower/safflower, peanut/groundnut oil or vegetable oil. These can all be heated to very high temperatures.
- Use fresh oil every time – used oil has impurities that affect the flavour of the food.
- Don't add too much food to the pan at once – this lowers the temperature of the oil and stops a crisp shell forming. It might also make the pan overflow. The larger the pieces, the fewer should go in at once.
- Do not cover the pan – this creates steam, which stops the food from becoming crisp.
- Tip fried food onto kitchen paper/paper towels to drain off the excess oil. Sprinkle immediately with sea salt for savoury foods, or sugar for sweet – to absorb excess fat and stop the food from tasting greasy.

drying heat

- If you don't have a cooking thermometer, test the heat of the oil by adding a cube of bread. If it browns in:

  60 seconds, 180°C (360°F), it's suitable for gentle frying, such as the first stage of cooking fries.

  40 seconds, 190°C (375°F), for moderately hot frying.

  20 seconds, 195°C (385°F), for hotter frying, the right temperature for tempura and the second frying of fries.

  10 seconds. This means it's too hot! Turn off the heat immediately.

safety rules

- Don't leave the pan unattended at any time – very hot oil needs to be watched carefully.
- Keep a heavy metal pan lid nearby in case the oil catches fire. If this does happen, turn the heat off immediately and slam on the lid.

salmon tempura

salmon tempura

Tempura batter shouldn't be smooth, so mix it very briefly, using chopsticks rather than a fork. Make the batter just before you use it.

2 eggs
150 ml/⅔ cup ice-cold sparkling mineral water
115 g/¾ cup plain/all-purpose flour
55 g/⅓ cup cornflour/cornstarch
3 tablespoons finely chopped chives
500 g/1 lb. salmon fillet, sliced crossways into 16 strips
sunflower/safflower oil, for deep-frying
deep-fat fryer, large saucepan or wok

CHILLI SAUCE
6 tablespoons sesame seeds, toasted (page 11)
3 red chillies/chiles, finely diced
2 tablespoons dark soy sauce
1 tablespoon white wine vinegar
1 tablespoon (runny) honey

serves 4

1 To make the sauce, put the sesame seeds and chillies/chiles in a bowl and add the soy sauce.

2 Add the vinegar and honey. Stir.

3 To make the batter, crack the eggs into a bowl.

4 Pour in the sparkling water and mix quickly.

5 Add the flours and stir briefly with chopsticks. Don't overmix – the batter should have lumps.

6 Add the chives and stir briefly. ⇨

7 Pour the oil into a deep-fat fryer, saucepan or wok and heat.

8 To test the heat of the oil, add a cube of white bread. If it browns in 20 seconds, the oil is ready for cooking. If you have a cooking thermometer, it should reach 195°C (385°F).

9 Dip the salmon pieces into the batter.

10 Add the salmon pieces to the pan, 3 at a time, and fry, in batches, for 2–3 minutes until golden.

11 Remove from the oil, drain on kitchen paper/paper towels and sprinkle with salt. Serve immediately with the chilli sauce.

TIPS FOR FRYING IN BATTER

• If making tempura (Japanese) batter, mix the batter at the very last moment, and mix it roughly so there are still quite a lot of lumps in it.

• To make other batters, follow the recipe, mix well, then set aside for about 30 minutes to allow the starch cells in the flour to expand – this will make the batter lighter.

• The Indian version of tempura is called bhaji or pakora – this batter contains gram flour made from chickpeas.

ELECTRIC DEEP-FAT FRYERS

• If you plan to deep-fry often, an electric fryer takes the guesswork out of oil temperatures. The machine heats the oil to the temperature you want, then automatically switches off.

• One of their advantages is that they fry with the lid on, which stops frying smells escaping.

• Always follow the manufacturer's instructions.

root vegetable chunky fries with herb mayo

Perfect fries are cooked twice, at two different temperatures – first to cook them through, then in hotter oil to make them brilliantly crisp and golden.

375 g/1 lb. sweet potatoes, cut into thick fries
375 g/1 lb. potatoes, cut into thick fries
375 g/1 lb. parsnips, cut into thick fries
sunflower/safflower oil, for frying
salt, to serve

HERB MAYO
a large bunch of coriander/cilantro, chopped
4 tablespoons mayonnaise
a squeeze of fresh lime juice
salt and freshly ground black pepper
deep-fat fryer or large saucepan

serves 4

Soak the vegetable fries in a bowl of cold water for 10 minutes to remove excess starch. Drain and dry well with a dish towel.

Meanwhile, put the coriander/cilantro and mayonnaise into a small food processor, add 1 tablespoon water and process until blended. Add lime juice and salt and pepper to taste.

Half fill a deep-fat fryer or large saucepan with oil and heat to about 180°C (360°F), or until a cube of bread browns in about 60 seconds. Working in 2–3 batches, plunge the vegetable chips into the oil and cook for 6–8 minutes, until cooked through but not golden. Remove and drain on kitchen paper/paper towels.

Increase the heat to about 195°C (385°F), or until a cube of bread browns in 20 seconds. Plunge the chips back into the oil and cook for 2–3 minutes until golden.

Remove, drain on kitchen paper/paper towels and sprinkle with salt. Serve at once with the herb mayo.

FRYING TIPS
• Cut the potatoes into chips, then soak in water for 10 minutes to remove the starch. Drain and pat dry on kitchen paper/paper towels.
• Fry fries in batches, to make sure the temperature of the oil remains constant.
• Fry first at 180°C (360°F) for 6–8 minutes.
• Drain on crumpled kitchen paper/paper towels, then increase the heat to 195°C (385°F) and fry until crisp and golden – the time will depend on the size of the fries, but 2–3 minutes is a guide.

grill pans

A stove-top grill pan is a ridged cast iron pan used on top of the stove to produce the intense, char-grilled flavours of a barbecue/grill. This simple tool is definitely one of my favourite ways of cooking – the heat of the pan sears the outside of food and cooks it through quickly. It's also a healthy way to cook, since the food sits on the ridges above the fat and not in it.

Grill pan tips

- Always preheat the stove-top grill pan, then add the food when it is very hot.

- Brush the food – not the pan – lightly with oil before cooking, to prevent sticking.

- When you have added the food, don't move it around. When it is ready to turn, it will come away easily from the pan without sticking.

- Serve straight from the pan. If left to cool, meat will toughen and vegetables will continue to cook and become soggy.

- Marinating food first with oils, herbs and spices enhances the flavour.

- Salt food after cooking not before – salt draws out the moisture and can give dry results.

- Delicate white fish and salmon will cook quickly, but to make sure they cook all the way through reduce the temperature a little.

- For thicker foods, such as chicken, put a weight on top to ensure even contact with the pan. A saucepan half-filled with water works well.

seared scallops with brittle prosciutto

Seared food is cooked quickly over high heat to seal the outside and form a nice crust. Scallops cook fast, and carry on cooking off the heat, so keep a careful watch on them – when overcooked, they are tough.

4 slices prosciutto
12 large scallops
125 g/2 cups salad leaves such as lamb's lettuce/corn salad
freshly ground black pepper

TO DRIZZLE
extra virgin olive oil
balsamic vinegar

serves 4

1   Heat a stove-top grill pan until very hot. Add the prosciutto and cook for 1–2 minutes on each side until crisp. Remove and set aside.

2   Grind black pepper over the scallops.

3   Add the scallops to the hot pan. Cook for 1–2 minutes on each side until opaque.

4   Divide the salad leaves between 4 plates.

5   Lightly drizzle with oil.

6   Drizzle with a little balsamic vinegar.

Top the salad with 3 scallops, then break over the brittle prosciutto. Sprinkle with pepper and serve at once.

seared scallops with brittle prosciutto

125 g/4$\frac{1}{2}$ oz. soft, mild goat cheese
salt and freshly ground black pepper

serves 4

Heat a stove-top grill pan until hot. Add the ciabatta and cook for 1–2 minutes on each side until lightly toasted and charred.

Meanwhile, put the salad leaves in a bowl, add the olive oil and salt and pepper to taste.

Spread the onion marmalade on the toasted ciabatta and put onto serving plates. Add a handful of salad and crumble the goat cheese on top. Sprinkle with olive oil and lots of black pepper.

lamb steaks with coriander cumin crust

Lamb, like duck, can throw off quite a bit of fat as it cooks. The grill pan keeps the meat up and out of the fat, which you can just pour off as it accumulates.

1 tablespoon cumin seeds
1 tablespoon coriander seeds
1 tablespoon cracked black pepper
4 tablespoons flat leaf parsley, coarsely chopped
4 lamb steaks, from the leg, 150 g/6 oz. each
1 tablespoon olive oil
200 g/1 cup Greek yogurt
3 tablespoons mint leaves, chopped
1 teaspoon freshly squeezed lemon juice
salt and freshly ground black pepper

serves 4

Crush the cumin and coriander seeds coarsely with a mortar and pestle or the back of a wooden spoon. Add the black pepper and parsley and stir to mix.

Rub the lamb steaks with the olive oil and coat each side with the parsley and spice mixture.

Heat a stove-top grill pan until hot, add the lamb and cook for 2–3 minutes on each side for rare or 4–5 minutes for medium, depending on thickness.

While the lamb is cooking, put the yogurt, mint and lemon juice in bowl, add salt and pepper to taste and mix well. Carve the steaks into thick slices and serve with the minted yogurt.

pan-grilled bruschetta with onion marmalade and goat cheese

pan-grilled bruschetta with onion marmalade and goat cheese

Char-grilled bread is more than just toast – it stays chewy on the inside, has a smoky flavour and lovely stripes from the grill pan.

2 ciabatta rolls, halved crossways
4 large handfuls of mixed salad leaves
1 tablespoon extra virgin olive oil, plus extra for serving
4 tablespoons red onion marmalade (page 145)

sweet teatime bruschetta

Bruschetta doesn't have to be bread – teacakes can also be toasted on the grill pan. Cook the fruit very briefly, so it just begins to soften and release its sweet juices, without becoming mushy.

2 teacakes/English muffins, halved
15 g/1 tablespoon unsalted butter
1 tablespoon (caster) sugar
250 g/2 cups medium strawberries,
    hulled and cut into quarters
250 g/2 cups raspberries
thick or clotted cream, to serve

serves 4

Heat a stove-top grill pan until hot. Add the teacake/muffin halves and cook for about 1 minute on each side until just lightly charred.

Heat the butter in a frying pan until melted. Add the sugar and strawberries and cook for about 1 minute, stirring frequently, until the sugar has dissolved. Add the raspberries and cook for 20–30 seconds. Put a teacake/muffin, cut side up, on each plate. Spoon over the fruit and serve with a dollop of cream.

trout with tarragon and bacon

barbecues

There are many kinds of outdoor barbecues/grills. Some people have electric or gas-fired grills. Others have a kettle-style grill on legs or wheels. For a smoky barbecue flavour, a wood-fired grill is required, but for nice charred surfaces – without the woodsmoke scent – grills with special briquettes or charcoal are very accessible.

preparing the barbecue/grill

- Preheat the barbecue/grill to the required temperature. To test, hold the palm of your hand 10 cm/4 inches from the heat. If you have to pull your hand away in 2 seconds, it's the right heat.

- If using charcoal or wood, never try to cook when there are still flames or the coals are still red – wait until they have a covering of light grey ash.

- If using charcoal or wood, keep the food 5 cm/2 inches away from the coals for thin cuts, such as kebabs/kabobs or fish, or up to 15 cm/6 inches for thick cuts which need to cook for longer.

- Have patience. Allow enough time for the barbecue/grill to reach the right heat. (Then allow enough time for the food to cook properly – food will take longer to cook on a barbecue/grill than by other means.)

barbecue cooking/grilling tips

- Cook foods over an even, medium heat. If the temperature is too high, the food will scorch and char on the outside and be raw on the inside.

- Cook beef or lamb at a higher heat than chicken or pork.

- If cooking on skewers, first oil them if they are metal or soak them in water for 30 minutes if they are bamboo.

- Trim excess fat – too much causes the coals to flare up and the food to burn.

- Marinating meat and fish before cooking enhances the flavour and tenderizes the flesh. Shake off the marinade before cooking so the liquid doesn't cause flare-ups.

- Don't prod and prick the food while it's cooking – this will release precious juices, cause flare-ups and cause the food to dry out.

- Use tongs and turn the food only once. Separate tongs should be used for raw and cooked foods.

- If cooking large pieces, start them off in the oven, otherwise the outside will be finished before the middle is cooked.

trout with tarragon and bacon

The bacon keeps the trout moist and stops it breaking up.

8 small trout fillets, skin removed
leaves from a bunch of tarragon
juice of 1 lemon
12 slices (rindless) bacon, stretched to allow
    for shrinkage
freshly ground black pepper

TO SERVE
4–5 tablespoons crème fraîche or sour cream
2–3 tablespoons wholegrain mustard
2 lemons, cut into wedges

serves 4

Put 4 of the trout fillets on a board and cover generously with tarragon. Sprinkle with lemon juice and black pepper. Top with the remaining fillets and wrap each pair in 3 slices of bacon to make 4 packages.

Put the crème fraîche and mustard in a bowl and mix gently. Transfer the trout packages to a preheated barbecue/grill and cook for about 5 minutes on each side until the bacon is crisp. Serve hot with the crème fraîche and mustard mixture and lemon wedges.

barbecue corn with spicy butter

If you can't find corn with the husks still attached, wrap them in foil before cooking. Other vegetables are also good cooked on the barbecue/grill – try whole (bell) peppers (and scrape off the burnt skin before serving), butternut squash or root vegetables like potatoes and carrots (wrapped in foil).

4 ears of corn, with husks

SPICY BUTTER
90 g/7 tablespoons salted butter
2 fresh chillies, seeded and finely chopped
a bunch of coriander/cilantro, coarsely chopped
grated zest and juice of 1 lime

serves 4

To make the spicy butter, put the butter, chillies, coriander/cilantro, lime zest and juice in a bowl and mix.

Put the corn on the preheated barbecue/grill and cook for about 15 minutes, turning occasionally, until charred all over.

To serve, pull back the husks from the corn, spread with a large spoonful of spicy butter and eat at once.

lemon spatchcocked chicken

Spatchcocked chickens have the backbones removed with scissors and are then opened out flat (buy ready-split or ask the butcher to do it). The chicken cooks through evenly, so is ideal for the barbecue/grill. Cook bony side down first – the bone transfers heat to the flesh.

2 lemons
3 tablespoons olive oil
1 chicken, 1.8 kg/4 lbs., split down the back and opened out flat
a handful of thyme sprigs
freshly ground black pepper

TO SERVE
quick aïoli (page 144)
1 lemon, cut into wedges
2 long metal skewers

serves 4

Using a zester, remove the zest from the lemons, leaving behind the white pith (which is very bitter). Cut the lemons in half and squeeze out the juice, reserving the squeezed halves.

Put the oil, lemon zest and juice in a large, shallow dish. Add plenty of black pepper and mix well. Add the split chicken, thyme and squeezed lemon halves, cover and refrigerate for 4–8 hours.

Remove the chicken to a board and discard the marinade. With the wings nearest you, push a skewer through 1 wing diagonally across the chicken and through the opposite leg. Push the second skewer diagonally through the second wing and leg. This will make the chicken easier to turn on the barbecue/grill.

Transfer to the preheated barbecue/grill – bony side down – and cook over medium coals for 20–25 minutes on each side, or until cooked through and lightly charred. Transfer the chicken to a clean wooden board, remove the skewers and serve with quick aïoli and lemon wedges.

lemon spatchcocked chicken

eggplant steaks with feta salad

Barbecues/cookouts often get a bit meat-heavy, so this is a refreshing change. It's a meal in itself, but it also goes well with lamb.

2 aubergines/eggplant, about 20 cm/8 inches, sliced diagonally
    into 2.5-cm/1-inch slices
4 tablespoons olive oil
grated zest of 1 lemon
2 tablespoons thyme leaves

eggplant steaks with feta salad

FETA SALAD

24 black olives, pitted and coarsely chopped

1 small red onion, diced

½ cucumber, diced

2 tomatoes, about 75 g/3 oz., diced

75 g/½ cup crumbled feta cheese

a bunch of flat leaf parsley, coarsely chopped

3 tablespoons olive oil

1 small garlic clove, crushed

juice of ½ lemon

salt and freshly ground black pepper

serves 4

Put the aubergine/eggplant slices, oil, lemon zest and thyme in a bowl. Toss to coat and add black pepper to taste. Set aside.

To make the salad, put the olives, onion, cucumber, tomatoes, feta, parsley, oil and garlic in a second bowl and mix gently. Set aside.

Cook the aubergine/eggplant on the preheated barbecue/grill or under a medium grill/broiler for about 5 minutes on each side until lightly charred and very soft. Sprinkle the salad with lemon juice, salt and pepper to taste. Divide the aubergine/eggplant and salad between 4 plates and serve.

seared swordfish with avocado and salsa

seared swordfish with avocado and salsa

Swordfish and tuna are perfect fish for the barbecue/grill – their texture is quite meat-like, so it doesn't fall apart.

2 tablespoons olive oil

grated zest and juice of 2 limes

4 swordfish steaks

2 large, just-ripe avocados, halved, pitted, peeled and sliced

freshly ground black pepper

SALSA

1 small red onion, chopped

1 red chilli, seeded and very finely chopped

1 large ripe tomato, halved, seeded (page 11) and chopped

3 tablespoons extra virgin olive oil

grated zest and juice of 1 lime

TO SERVE

1 lime, cut into wedges

a bunch of coriander/cilantro, chopped

serves 4

Put the oil, lime zest and juice into a small bowl and whisk well. Add plenty of black pepper. Put the swordfish steaks in a shallow dish and pour over the oil and lime mixture, making sure the fish is coated on all sides. Cover and refrigerate for up to 1 hour.

Meanwhile, to make the salsa, put the onion, chilli, tomato, oil, lime zest and juice in a bowl. Mix gently, then cover and refrigerate.

Heat the barbecue/grill to hot and cook the fish for about 2–3 minutes on each side or until just cooked through. Divide the avocado and fish between 4 plates, spoon over the salsa, sprinkle with coriander/cilantro and serve with lime wedges.

char-grilled steak with sizzled shrimp

If you can't find the extra large shrimp, use smaller ones, but to make them easier to turn on the barbecue/grill, remove the shell and slide them onto bamboo skewers. Remember to presoak the skewers in water so that they don't catch fire.

12 extra large uncooked, unpeeled prawns/shrimp
2 tablespoons (runny) honey
2 tablespoons olive oil
1 garlic clove, sliced
juice of ½ lime or lemon
4 sirloin steaks
2 tablespoons teriyaki sauce
freshly ground black pepper
chunky guacamole (page 143), to serve

serves 4

Put the prawns/shrimp in a shallow dish. Put the honey, oil, garlic and lime or lemon juice in a bowl and mix well. Pour the mixture over the prawns/shrimp and sprinkle with pepper. Cover and chill for 30 minutes to marinate.

Put the steaks on a plate and sprinkle with the teriyaki sauce. Transfer the steaks to a high heat on the barbecue/grill and sear for 2–3 minutes on each side for rare, 3–4 minutes for medium and 5–6 minutes for well-done, depending on thickness.

Remove the prawns/shrimp from their marinade and cook on the hot barbecue/grill for 1–2 minutes on each side, until pink and lightly charred. Brush with the marinade from time to time during cooking.

Put a steak onto each serving plate and put a few prawns/shrimp on top. Serve with the chunky guacamole.

hot boozy berry desserts

These desserts need only a gentle heat to cook, so put them on the barbecue/grill last of all, after the coals have died down. The double foil squares not only give extra strength to avoid punctures, but also stop the bottoms of the muffins from scorching as they heat through.

4 blueberry muffins
125 g/1 cup blueberries
125 g/1 cup raspberries
125 ml/½ cup sweet wine, such as Sauternes or Muscat
250 g/1 cup mascarpone cheese
grated zest and juice of 1 orange
icing/confectioners' sugar
8 pieces of foil, 25 cm/10 inches square

serves 4

Cut the muffins in half diagonally from top to bottom. Put the 2 halves of each muffin on a double layered square of foil and scrunch the foil round the base and up the sides of the muffins to keep the 2 halves loosely together and hold them in place, leaving enough room to sandwich berries in the middle.

Divide the blueberries and raspberries between the sliced muffin halves. Pour a quarter of the sweet wine over each muffin and bring the foil together tightly to seal the muffins in a package. Cook on the barbecue/grill for about 5–7 minutes, or until steaming hot. Take care when testing or eating them, as the fruit in the middle gets much hotter than the muffins.

Meanwhile, put the mascarpone in a bowl and beat with a wooden spoon until soft. Add the orange zest and juice and icing/confectioners' sugar to taste. Transfer the packages to plates, open them up and serve hot, topped with the orange mascarpone.

COOKING MEAT ON THE BARBECUE/GRILL

• Cook at a high heat first, to seal the outside, then transfer to a cooler part of the grill to cook the inside to your liking.

• Don't cook very thick cuts, or the outside will be overcooked before the inside is done. Make them no more than about 5 cm/2 inches.

• When cooking pork (and also chicken), make sure it is thoroughly cooked, with no sign of pink in the middle (to check, stick a skewer through the thickest part – the juices should run clear or golden, with no trace of pink).

• Finish cooking in the oven if necessary.

hot boozy berry desserts

grilling

As much as I love the trend these days for grill pans and barbecuing, I try not to let the simple grill/broiler at the top of my oven become a forgotten tool. The overhead heat produces a lovely char-grill texture on the outside. It also allows the fat to drain off the food into the tray/pan below, so is a healthy way to cook.

grilling/broiling tips

- Preheat the grill/broiler to its highest setting until very hot, then adjust the heat according to the recipe. Preheating is essential to seal the outside of meat properly, leaving the middle succulent.

- Tender cuts of meat, such as fillet steaks, lamb cutlets or chicken breast, are best for grilling/broiling.

- Use thin cuts, not more than 5 cm/2 inches thick, for grilling, so that the meat can cook through without the outside burning.

- Don't prod the food with a fork while it is cooking under the grill/broiler – you will lose its lovely juices.

- When grilling/broiling thick pieces of chicken, or sausages, turn them often with tongs or a spoon and fork, so that they cook through without the surface drying out or burning.

- Keep a constant watch on food as it grills/broils – it is close to the heat and cooks very quickly. If it does cook too fast, lower the grill/pan tray so that it is further away from the heat.

- Marinating meat, fish and vegetables before cooking keeps them moist and adds flavour.

- Don't season with salt before grilling, as salt draws out moisture – do it during or after.

venison sausages with port
and cranberry ragout

venison sausages with port and cranberry ragout

Grilling/broiling is the healthy way to cook sausages, with the fat draining away into the grill/broiler tray. They are also less likely to split than if you pan-fry them. Turn them often, so that they cook through and brown evenly on the outside. You can make this with any good-quality sausages, but the gamey venison goes particularly well with the rich, red sauce.

2 large leeks, cut into 5-mm/¼-inch slices
25 g/2 tablespoons butter
1 tablespoon plain/all-purpose flour
1 tablespoon sugar
300 ml/1¼ cups red wine
3 tablespoons port
150 ml/⅔ cup chicken or vegetable stock
a large sprig of rosemary
8 good-quality sausages, preferably venison
250 g/2 cups fresh or frozen cranberries
salt and freshly ground black pepper
mustard mash (page 17), to serve

serves 4

Rinse the leeks well in a bowl of cold water, to remove any grit or dirt, then drain in a sieve/strainer. Melt the butter in a large saucepan. Add the leeks and gently fry over medium heat, stirring frequently, for 8–10 minutes until softened and slightly golden.

Preheat the grill/broiler to a medium setting.

Add the flour to the saucepan of fried leeks and cook, stirring, for 1 minute. Add the sugar, wine, port, stock, rosemary and plenty of salt and pepper. Bring to the boil, reduce the heat and simmer for about 15–20 minutes.

Meanwhile, put the sausages on the grill/broiler tray and cook, turning them frequently, for 15–20 minutes until browned all over and cooked all the way through.

Add the cranberries to the saucepan and simmer for a further 5–6 minutes until they begin to soften and pop. Add salt, pepper and sugar to taste, then serve with the sausages and mustard mash.

charred paprika chicken

Cutting slashes into the surface of the chicken speeds up the grilling/broiling time while keeping it moist and tender. The butter mixture runs into the grooves and bastes the chicken.

4 chicken breasts, with skin and bone
50 g/4 tablespoons butter
4 tablespoons wholegrain mustard
2 teaspoons honey
1 tablespoon sweet paprika
freshly squeezed juice of 1 lemon
salt and freshly ground black pepper
sour cream, to serve

serves 4

Preheat the grill/broiler to a medium setting. Using a sharp knife, cut 3 slashes diagonally through the chicken skin and flesh to the bone.

Put the butter, mustard, honey and paprika into a bowl and mix well. Brush the skinless side of the chicken with half the butter mixture and put under the grill/broiler for 7–8 minutes. Turn the chicken over, brush with the remaining mixture, and return to the grill/broiler for a further 7–8 minutes until cooked through.

Remove the chicken from the grill/broiler and sprinkle with the lemon juice. Arrange on a large dish and serve with sour cream.

simple charred peppers

Grilling/broiling (bell) peppers is one of the best ways to skin them. It also brings out their sweetness. Try these squashed onto crusty bread, mixed into freshly cooked pasta, or tossed with rocket/arugula and Parmesan shavings as a salad.

1 red (bell) pepper, quartered and seeded
1 (bell) orange pepper, quartered and seeded
1 (bell) yellow pepper, quartered and seeded
4 tablespoons extra virgin olive oil
2 teaspoons balsamic vinegar
1 tablespoon fresh basil leaves
salt and freshly ground black pepper

serves 4

Preheat the grill/broiler to a medium setting.

Put the pepper quarters on the grill/broiler tray, cut side down. Put under the grill/broiler for about 5–8 minutes until the skins are charred and blackened. Remove the peppers to a plastic freezer bag, seal and set aside to cool. The steam inside the bag will loosen the skins and make them easy to scrape off and remove.

Take the cooled peppers out of the bag, then peel and scrape away the charred skin. Discard any juices from the bag.

Put the peppers into a shallow dish. Drizzle with the olive oil and balsamic vinegar. Add salt and pepper to taste and sprinkle with the basil. Cover and set aside at room temperature for 2 hours before serving, for the peppers to soak up the dressing.

whole roasted chicken with prunes and thyme

roasting

Roasting is like baking, and cooks the food by indirect heat in a dry enclosed atmosphere, making the outside crisp and the inside tender. Centuries ago, roasting of meat was done in front of an open fire on a turning spit. It's much easier now – all you need is an oven and a roasting pan.

roasting tips

- Always preheat the oven to the correct temperature before adding the food.
- Use a good-quality, heavy-gauge roasting pan.
- Meat and poultry cook more quickly if they include the bones. Always follow the recipe and test towards the end of cooking time.
- Some foods, especially chicken or pheasant, can dry out in the oven. Putting streaky/fatty bacon over the breast protects the meat and keeps it moist.
- "Basting" means spooning the pan juices over the food while roasting. Baste or turn the food about every 30 minutes. Don't over-baste or you will lower the oven temperature and the estimated cooking time will be altered. Meat with a good layer of fat needs less basting.
- To brown roasted vegetables evenly, shake or toss them halfway through the cooking time.
- Some vegetables – potatoes, fennel, and parsnips – are best par-boiled (page 15) before roasting.

times and temperatures

- Weigh meat and roast using the times given on this page as a guide. However, remember that if the piece of meat is long and thin rather than thick and fat, it will take less time.
- Chicken and duck: 200°C (400°F) Gas 6 for 20 minutes per 500 g/pound, plus 20 minutes.
- Pork: without crackling/skin, 170°C (325°F) Gas 3 for 40 minutes per 500 g/pound. If cooking pork with crackling/skin, 220°C (425°F) Gas 7 for 30 minutes then at 190°C (375°F) Gas 5 for 20 minutes per 500 g/pound.
- Lamb and beef: first seal the outside by frying or roasting at the highest possible temperature for 20 minutes. Then cook at 190°C (375°F) Gas 5:
rare: 15 minutes per 500 g/pound
medium: 20 minutes per 500 g/pound
well done: 25 minutes per 500 g/pound

roast loin of pork with butter-baked apples and cider gravy

When roasting pork with crackling, you start it off in a very hot oven to crackle the skin, then reduce the temperature for the meat to cook more gently.

2.25 kg/5 lbs. loin of pork, with skin
olive oil
coarse sea salt

CIDER GRAVY
1 tablespoon plain/all-purpose flour
150 ml/⅔ cup cider
300 ml/1¼ cups chicken stock
salt and freshly ground black pepper

serves 6

Preheat the oven to 220°C (425°F) Gas 7.

Using a large, sharp knife, score the pork skin at 5-mm/ ¼-inch intervals, cutting through the skin but not right through the fat. This stops the skin from shrinking and turns it into crackling. You can buy pork ready-scored, or ask your butcher to do it for you.

1 Brush the pork skin with oil and sprinkle generously with salt.

2 Rub the oil and salt into the skin.

Transfer to a roasting pan and put in the oven. Roast for 30 minutes, then reduce the oven temperature to 190°C (375°F) Gas 5 and roast for a further 2 hours until the meat is cooked through and the skin has crackled.

3 Transfer the pork to a carving board and cover well with foil. Set aside to rest while you make the gravy.

4 Tip off as much of the fat as possible from the roasting pan, keeping all the meat juices underneath the fat. Put the roasting pan over a high heat, add the flour and stir well to mix.

5 Cook, stirring constantly with a wooden spoon, until the flour has turned brown.

6 Remove from the heat, then add the cider and stock. Stir quickly, then mix with a whisk. Return to the heat and bring to the boil, whisking all the time. Reduce the heat and simmer for 2 minutes. Add salt and pepper to taste and pour into a jug/sauceboat.

7 Uncover the pork and remove the layer of crackling. Carve the flesh into slices and cut the crackling into pieces. Serve hot with butter-baked apples (page 82) and the cider gravy.

4

5

6

7

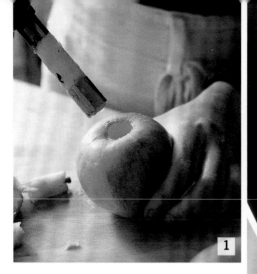

butter-baked apples

6 large, tart dessert apples
50 g/4 tablespoons unsalted butter
2 tablespoons finely chopped fresh sage
1 garlic clove, crushed
2 tablespoons Demerara/brown sugar, plus extra
    for sprinkling
150 ml/⅔ cup dry cider
freshly ground black pepper

serves 6

1 Using a corer, remove the core of each apple.

2 Score a ring around the middle of each apple with a sharp knife, to stop the apples bursting as they cook. Transfer to an ovenproof dish or roasting pan.

3 Put the butter, sage, garlic and sugar in a bowl.

4 Beat with a wooden spoon to mix, adding freshly ground black pepper to taste.

5 Spoon the sage butter into the cavity of each apple and sprinkle sugar over the top.

6 Pour the cider into the roasting pan.

7 Put the apples into the oven 35 minutes before the pork is cooked and bake for 30–35 minutes until soft all the way through but still keeping their shape. Serve with the roast pork and cider gravy.

whole roasted chicken with prunes and thyme

To baste the chicken a few times as it cooks, spoon the wine juices over the top. Basting keeps the food moist. To test for doneness, use a small knife or skewer to pierce the fattest part of the leg through to the bone – it is cooked when the juices that run out are clear and there is no trace of pink.

1 chicken, about 1.8 kg/4 lbs.
4 red onions, peeled and cut into 6 wedges
250 g/1½ cups ready-to-eat, pitted prunes
600 ml/2¾ cups red wine
1 teaspoon (caster) sugar
a bunch of thyme sprigs
25 g/2 tablespoons butter
salt and freshly ground black pepper

serves 4

Preheat the oven to 200°C (400°F) Gas 6.

Loosely tie the legs of the chicken with string to keep its plump shape while cooking. Sprinkle with salt and pepper and put in a large roasting pan. Put the onions and prunes around the chicken and pour the wine over the top. Sprinkle with the sugar and thyme sprigs. Dot the butter over the chicken, transfer to the preheated oven and roast for about 1½ hours, basting frequently, until the chicken is dark golden brown and the juices run clear.

Move to a board, carve and serve with the onions and prunes.

roasted potatoes

You can roast potatoes in other oils, such as sunflower/safflower, or even in lard, but olive oil is much the healthiest, and delicious with it. The sprinkled flour gives the perfect coating to make the outsides crisp. If you don't have rock salt, which is very coarse and adds extra crunch, use sea salt.

1 kg/2 lbs. potatoes, cut into 5-cm/2-inch pieces
150 ml/⅔ cup olive oil
25 g/2 tablespoons butter
1 tablespoon plain/all-purpose flour, seasoned with rock salt
    and freshly ground black pepper

serves 4

Preheat the oven to 220°C (425°F) Gas 7.

Put the potatoes into a large saucepan and cover with cold water. Cover with a lid and bring to the boil. Reduce the heat and simmer for 8 minutes to par-boil.

Meanwhile, pour the olive oil into a roasting pan and add the butter. Put into the oven for 5 minutes, until smoking hot.

Drain the potatoes well and return them to the saucepan. Holding the lid on, shake the pan well to roughen the surface of the potatoes. Remove the roasting pan from the oven, add the potatoes and turn them over with a large metal spoon to coat them all over with oil. Sprinkle with the flour, then roast for about 45–50 minutes until crisp and golden. Use a large, metal spoon to push the potatoes around the pan from time to time during cooking, to prevent them from sticking.

orange roasted roots

Roasting butternuts, carrots and sweet potatoes until they caramelize is a fantastic way to bring out their natural sweetness and intense flavours.

1 butternut squash
4 carrots, halved lengthways
8 shallots
2 sweet potatoes, cut into wedges
1 orange, halved crossways
4 tablespoons olive oil
2 large sprigs of rosemary
8 garlic cloves
salt and freshly ground black pepper

serves 4

Preheat the oven to 200°C (400°F) Gas 6. Cut the butternut in half lengthways and peel, using a small, sharp knife. Scoop out the seeds with a metal spoon and discard. Put the cut halves, flat side down, on a board and cut into chunks, about 5 cm/2 inches.

Put the butternut, carrots, shallots and sweet potatoes into a large roasting pan. Squeeze over the juice from the orange and put the squeezed halves into the pan with the vegetables. Drizzle with the olive oil and put the rosemary on top. Add plenty of salt and black pepper, then transfer to the preheated oven and roast for 20 minutes.

Remove from the oven and add the garlic. Shake the pan and move the vegetables around to stop them sticking. Return them to the oven for a further 20 minutes until tender and slightly caramelized.

WHICH VEGETABLES ARE GOOD FOR ROASTING?

• All root vegetables are good roasted – potatoes, carrots, parsnips, beetroot, sweet potatoes and turnips.
• Most of the onion family – including onions (whole, halved or in wedges), shallots (eschallots), and garlic. Roast garlic heads whole or separate into (unpeeled) cloves. Guests can peel the cloves before they eat them.
• Starchy vegetables like pumpkin and butternut squash.
• Squashy ones like (bell) peppers, courgettes/zucchini and aubergines/eggplant.
• Tomatoes – cut them in half and roast them cut side up. I love to serve roasted tomatoes with a few olives added towards the end of roasting time.

---

saffron fish roast

Roasted vegetables make a delicious base for grilled/broiled fish in this recipe. You can roast rather than grill/broil the fish too, but remember that it will take a very short time, so cook it just until the flesh turns opaque.

2 red onions, cut into wedges
2 red (bell) peppers, halved, seeded and each half cut into 3
500 g/1 lb. new potatoes
1 tablespoon olive oil
250 g/8 oz. baby plum tomatoes
500 g/1 lb. thick, skinless cod fillet, cut into 4 chunks
500 g/1 lb. thick, skinless salmon fillet, cut into 4 slices
½ teaspoon rock or sea salt
1 lemon, cut into wedges, to serve

MARINADE
a pinch of saffron threads
4 tablespoons finely chopped flat leaf parsley
2 tablespoons extra virgin olive oil
freshly ground black pepper

serves 4

Preheat the oven to 200°C (400°F) Gas 6. Put the saffron in a small bowl, add 3 tablespoons boiling water and set aside to soak.

Put the onions, (bell) peppers and potatoes into a large roasting pan. Add the olive oil with salt and pepper to taste and mix well. Transfer to the preheated oven and roast for about 45 minutes, until the vegetables are cooked and slightly charred. Add the tomatoes to the pan and roast for a further 5 minutes.

Meanwhile, to make the marinade, put the saffron and its soaking water into a large bowl, add the remaining marinade ingredients and mix. Put the fish into a shallow dish and pour over the marinade. Cover and refrigerate until needed.

Preheat the grill/broiler to medium heat. Remove the fish from its marinade and discard the marinade. Put the fish on top of the vegetables in the roasting pan. Sprinkle with the rock or sea salt and cook under the grill/broiler for 10–12 minutes, until the fish is just cooked through.

Divide the fish and vegetables between 4 large serving plates and serve with the lemon wedges.

saffron fish roast

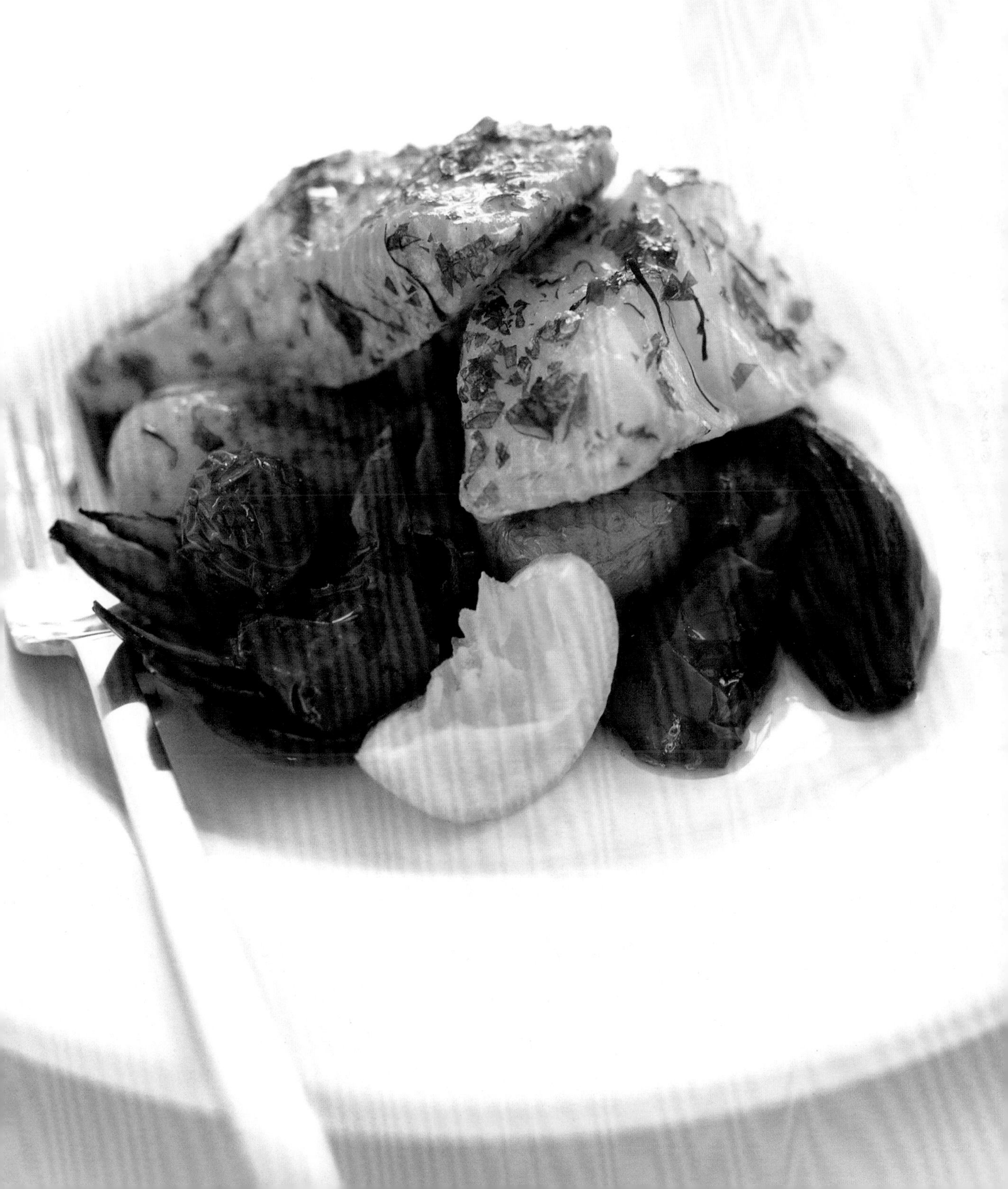

braising

Braising is a variation on poaching. This chapter covers both braising (cooking in just a little liquid) and stewing (cooking in a lot of liquid). The food stews very slowly in an enclosed dish in the oven or on top of the stove, until it becomes very tender, and the sauce and juices rich and flavourful. Curries, stews and spicy tagines are all wonderful examples and very simple to make – once they are in the dish, they more or less look after themselves.

braising tips

- Use a heavy saucepan or flameproof casserole dish with a well-fitting lid, or a wok for quick braises.

- Trim excess fat from your meat and, if using pieces, make sure they are equally sized so that they cook evenly.

- Many recipes sear the meat and vegetables for a braise before adding the liquid. Searing is done by frying in a pan until all the surfaces are sealed and lightly browned. This produces caramelized flavours and keeps the juices in.

- Don't add too much salt at the beginning, as flavours will become more intense as they cook. You can always add more at the end if necessary.

- Add robust herbs – such as thyme, rosemary and bay leaves – at the beginning of cooking and more delicate herbs – such as coriander/cilantro, basil and parsley – at the last moment.

- Bring the liquid to the boil first, then immediately reduce the heat to just a gentle simmer.

- Keep the temperature constant – braising is a slow method of cooking, so the heat needs to be even and gentle.

- Keep an eye on the level of the liquid in the pan or dish and top it up if necessary – it doesn't have to be stock or wine, often water will do.

reheating

- Braised dishes often taste better if made the day before and reheated. Keep them in the refrigerator overnight and remove any fat from the surface before reheating thoroughly on top of the stove or in the oven.

- Heat them to boiling point first on top of the stove, then transfer to a preheated oven and cook at 160°C (325°F) Gas 3 for about 30 minutes, so the dish is heated right through.

chicken korma with almonds and cream

This mild Indian curry is a typical example of a braise. The spices are fried first to release their aromas, before the other ingredients are added.

3 tablespoons sunflower/safflower oil

2 large onions, finely sliced

2 large garlic cloves, crushed

1 tablespoon turmeric

2 teaspoons ground coriander

2 teaspoons ground cumin

10 cardamom pods

1 teaspoon black pepper, cracked

¼ teaspoon freshly grated nutmeg

6 large boneless, skinless, chicken thighs, halved

600 ml/2¾ cups chicken stock

juice of 1 lemon

1 bay leaf

150 ml/⅔ cup double/heavy cream

2 tablespoons ground almonds

2 tablespoons mint, shredded

cooked basmati rice or naan bread, to serve

serves 4

1 Heat 2 tablespoons of the oil in a large, flameproof casserole dish or wok. Add the onions and fry gently for 15 minutes until softened and beginning to brown.

2 Add the garlic and spices to the onions and fry for about 1 minute. Frying spices releases their aroma. Use your nose to tell how long to fry them – they give a burst of fragrance when they are ready.

3 Heat the remaining oil in a large frying pan and add the chicken pieces.

4 Fry for 2 minutes on each side or until golden, then transfer to the casserole dish.

5 Add the stock.

6 Add the lemon juice and bay leaf.

7 Bring to the boil.

8 Reduce the heat, cover with a lid and simmer gently for 20–25 minutes until the chicken is cooked through.

9 Add the cream, ground almonds and mint and simmer for a further 2 minutes. Serve hot with basmati rice (page 22) or warmed naan bread.

bean, bacon and rosemary ragout

Heat the oil in a large, heavy-based saucepan. Add the onion and cook for 5 minutes until golden.

Add the bacon to the pan and cook, stirring from time to time, for a further 4–5 minutes, until crisp. Add the garlic and cook for another minute. Add the canned and cherry tomatoes, vinegar and sugar. Stir, then bring to the boil. Reduce the heat and simmer for 5 minutes.

Add the cannellini and borlotti beans and the rosemary. Simmer for another 5 minutes until bubbling hot. Add salt and freshly ground black pepper to taste.

Ladle the ragout into 4 large soup plates. Top with a handful of spinach or rocket/arugula. Drizzle with olive oil and balsamic vinegar, sprinkle with black pepper and serve with crusty bread.

BROWNING VEGETABLES

• Many recipes, especially Western and Indian dishes, brown the vegetables in oil or butter at the beginning of a braise.

• This is done to caramelize the natural sugars in the vegetables – it gives more delicious flavour to the dish.

---

bean, bacon and rosemary ragout

Canned beans make a hearty, speedy, stove-top braise. Unlike dried beans, they don't need to be soaked and cooked for hours, making this a fast dish to prepare. For vegetarians, omit the bacon and add 125 g/1 cup sliced fresh shiitake mushrooms at the same time as the onion.

1 tablespoon olive oil

1 large onion, coarsely chopped

125 g/4 slices thick-cut bacon, cubed

2 garlic cloves, crushed

800 g/18 oz. (2 cans) canned chopped tomatoes

250 g/2 cups cherry tomatoes

1 tablespoon balsamic vinegar

½ teaspoon sugar

400 g/14 oz. canned cannellini beans, drained and rinsed

400 g/14 oz. canned borlotti beans, drained and rinsed

1 tablespoon chopped fresh rosemary

salt and freshly ground black pepper

TO SERVE

young leaf spinach or rocket/arugula

extra virgin olive oil

balsamic vinegar

crusty bread

serves 4

green thai vegetable curry

This is a super-quick poach-braise – it cooks just long enough for the vegetables to become tender.

3 tablespoons green Thai curry paste

400 ml/1¾ cups canned coconut milk

425 ml/1¾ cups vegetable stock

1 large potato, cut into 2.5-cm/1-inch pieces

250 g/1 cup broccoli florets

250 g/1 cup cauliflower florets

125 g/1 cup frozen petit pois

125 g/1 cup sugar snap peas, halved lengthways

TO SERVE

1 lime, cut into wedges

cooked Thai fragrant rice (page 22)

serves 4

Put the curry paste in a wok, heat and cook for 2 minutes, stirring. Add the coconut milk, stock and potato. Bring to the boil, reduce the heat and simmer for 5 minutes. Add the broccoli and cauliflower florets, stalk end down, cover with a lid and simmer for 4 minutes. Add the peas and sugar snaps and cook for a further 2 minutes until all the vegetables are tender.

Ladle the curry into 4 bowls and serve with lime wedges and Thai fragrant rice.

green thai vegetable curry

beef braised in red wine with light gruyère dumplings

A classic stew – after being seared and browned, the meat cooks very slowly in the oven, giving it time to become beautifully tender and succulent.

20 g/1 oz. dried porcini mushrooms, thoroughly rinsed

2 tablespoons olive oil

1 kg/2 lbs. braising beef, cut into 4-cm/1½-inch chunks

425 ml/1¾ cups red wine

250 g/5 shallots, peeled and halved lengthways

3 large, open mushrooms, each cut into 8 wedges

1 tablespoon plain/all-purpose flour

1 bay leaf

1 tablespoon thyme leaves

GRUYÈRE DUMPLINGS

225 g/1½ cups plain/all-purpose flour

¼ teaspoon salt

2½ teaspoons baking powder

55 g/½ cup grated Gruyère cheese

3 tablespoons coarsely chopped flat leaf parsley

3 tablespoons chopped chives

2 tablespoons extra virgin olive oil

150 ml/⅔ cup milk

salt and freshly ground black pepper

serves 4

Preheat the oven to 150°C (300°F) Gas 2. Put the porcini in a bowl, cover with 600 ml/2¾ cups boiling water and let soak.

Meanwhile, heat 1 tablespoon of the oil in a large frying pan. Add half the beef and sear on all sides until brown. Using a slotted spoon, remove the beef from the pan and reserve. Repeat with the remaining beef. Add a good splash of the wine to the pan, stir well with a wooden spoon to remove the sediment, then pour into a bowl and reserve.

Add the remaining oil to the pan. When hot, add the shallots and fry for 4–5 minutes until golden brown. Add the open mushrooms and fry for a further 4–5 minutes. Sprinkle in the flour and cook, stirring continuously, for 1–2 minutes.

Pour in the remaining wine and reserved beef juices and add the reserved chunks of beef. Add the bay leaf, thyme and porcini with the liquid it has been soaking in. Bring to the boil and transfer to a medium-sized shallow casserole dish. Cover with a lid and cook in the oven for 2 hours.

To make the dumplings, 10 minutes before the 2 hours are up, sift the flour, salt and baking powder into a large bowl. Stir in the Gruyère, 2 tablespoons each of the parsley and chives and plenty of pepper. Add the oil and milk and stir lightly with a fork to form a soft dough.

Transfer the mixture to a floured surface and knead very lightly. Using floured hands, shape into 8 dumplings. Remove the stew from the oven and put the dumplings on top. Return to the oven and cook, uncovered, for 35–40 minutes more, until the dumplings have risen and are golden brown. Sprinkle with the remaining parsley and chives and serve hot.

moroccan lamb tagine

A tagine is a North African stew cooked in a tall, conical pot of the same name. It is traditionally cooked over an open fire, but it also works well cooked in the oven, or in a wok or sauté pan on top of the stove.

1 kg/2 lbs. boneless shoulder of lamb, trimmed of about half its fat and cut into 5-cm/2-inch chunks

600 ml/2⅔ cups chicken stock

2 tablespoons olive oil

1 large onion, coarsely chopped

4 garlic cloves, chopped

1 tablespoon ground cumin

1 tablespoon ground coriander

1 tablespoon hot paprika

400 g/14 oz. canned chopped tomatoes

1 cinnamon stick, broken in half

175 g/1 cup dried apricots

½ teaspoon freshly ground black pepper

3 large pieces of orange zest

TO SERVE

couscous or cracked wheat (page 141)

50 g/½ cup pine nuts, lightly toasted (page 11)

ORANGE RELISH

2 oranges, separated into segments

1 red onion, chopped

1 red chilli, finely chopped (page 43)

leaves from a bunch of coriander/cilantro

1 tablespoon mint leaves, finely sliced

serves 4

Heat a large, non-stick sauté pan or wok until hot. Add half the lamb chunks and sear on all sides until brown.

Using a slotted spoon, remove the browned lamb from the pan, put it on a plate and set aside. Add about 100 ml/½ cup of the chicken stock to the sauté pan or wok. Stir with a wooden spoon to remove all the flavourful sediment from the bottom, then pour out into a bowl and reserve. Add the remaining lamb to the pan and sear until brown, repeating the chicken stock process.

Return the pan to the heat and add the oil. When hot, add the onion and fry gently for about 10 minutes until golden. Add the garlic and fry for a further 2 minutes. Add the cumin, ground coriander and paprika to the pan and fry for a further minute. Add the reserved browned lamb and the tomatoes, cinnamon, apricots, pepper, orange zest and remaining stock.

Bring to the boil and cover with a lid. Reduce the heat and simmer very gently for about 2 hours until the meat is meltingly tender.

Put all the relish ingredients in a bowl and mix.

Serve the tagine sprinkled with pine nuts, accompanied by the relish and couscous or cracked wheat.

Note If cooking in the oven, use an ovenproof casserole dish and follow the recipe up to the point where the dish is covered with a lid. Then transfer to a preheated oven and cook at 150°C (300°F) Gas 2 for about 2 hours, or until the meat is very tender.

moroccan lamb tagine

baking

Cakes, scones and cookies, brownies and muffins, breads and pizzas, pies and tarts – it's all baking. They're mostly simple – try the samples in this chapter, then some of those in the chapter beginning on page 146. All you need is an oven and a few basic items of bakeware, listed on page 8.

baking tips

- Weigh and measure all the ingredients before you start to bake. Using accurate amounts is crucial to successful baking.

- Preheat the oven to the correct temperature before putting anything in it. If you're making pizza, preheat the baking sheet or pizza stone as well.

- Bread bakes best at a high heat, so that it rises and develops a nice crust – put it on the top shelf of the oven.

- Cakes are more delicate, so bake them at a lower temperature on the middle shelf of the oven.

- Bread can be made without yeast (page 99). The results are different from yeast-baked breads, but are just as good. Yeast-free bread doesn't keep as long, and is best eaten the day it is made.

- When making open pies, tarts and quiches (page 106) blind-bake the pastry shells. To bake blind means to line a tart pan with pastry, then with paper. Add dried beans or uncooked rice (or special ceramic baking beans) then bake until no longer transparent in a preheated oven at 200°C (400°F) Gas 6. Remove from the oven, remove the paper and beans or rice, then return to the oven for 3–5 minutes to dry out. This will make sure the pastry is cooked and crisp.

- When making pastry, wrap and chill the dough for 20–30 minutes before rolling out. The dough heats up as you are working on it – chilling allows it to cool and rest so it won't shrink too much while cooking.

- Remove baked goods from their pans as soon as they come out of the oven and put them on a wire rack to cool – that way, no soggy bottoms!

orange and bitter chocolate muffins

Muffins need room to grow, so fill the muffin pans only three-quarters full.

280 g/1¾ cups plain/all-purpose flour
1½ teaspoons baking powder
1 teaspoon salt
½ teaspoon bicarbonate of/baking soda
225 g/1 cup (caster) sugar
100 g/3 oz. dark/bittersweet chocolate (at least 70% cocoa solids)
1 orange
55 g/4 tablespoons butter
175 ml/¾ cup milk
12-hole muffin pan, preferably non-stick, lightly buttered

serves 12

Preheat the oven to 190°C (375°F) Gas 5.

1 Sift the flour, baking powder, salt and bicarbonate of/baking soda into a large bowl. Stir in the sugar.

2 Coarsely chop the chocolate.

3 Add the chocolate to the bowl and mix.

4 Make a well in the centre of the dry ingredients.

5 Using the fine setting on a box grater, grate the zest from the orange and set aside. Cut the orange in half crossways. Squeeze the juice from the orange halves.

6 Put the butter into a small saucepan and heat until melted. Pour into a second bowl.

7 Add milk and orange juice to the butter.

8 Pour the butter and orange mixture into the well of the dry ingredients. Stir briefly with a wooden spoon. Don't overmix – it should be lumpy, not smooth.

9 Spoon the mixture into the buttered pan. Bake in the preheated oven for about 20 minutes until golden and cooked through. (Insert a skewer into the middle of one muffin to test – when it is cooked the skewer will come out clean.)

10 Remove from the oven and let cool for a couple of minutes in the pan.

11 Remove from the pan to a wire rack and serve warm or at room temperature.

GREASING, FLOURING AND LINING BAKING PANS

• "Greasing" means brushing the inside of the pan with a thin film of butter or oil. This stops the food from sticking to the pan when cooked.

• Pans are sometimes then dusted with a light layer of flour, or lined with baking parchment on the base, or on the base and sides – also to stop the food sticking.

• Lining is usually done if the food is to be baked for a long time – say a large fruit cake.

Note For cooking, use best-quality cooking chocolate with at least 70% cocoa solids (listed on the wrapper).

black olive pizza crust

Once you have baked the pizza base from the recipe below, you can add whatever you fancy to the cooked crust – try some of the delicious toppings suggested here. They don't need any extra cooking – just top and serve!

225 g/1½ cups strong white bread flour

3.5 g (half a sachet/package) easy-blend/active dried yeast

2 tablespoons olive oil, plus extra for drizzling

85 g/½ cup black olives, pitted and chopped

2 garlic cloves, crushed

3 plum tomatoes, sliced crossways

1 teaspoon (caster) sugar

a baking sheet or pizza stone, lightly floured

serves 2

Sift the flour into a large bowl and stir in the yeast. Make a well in the centre of the flour, add about 125 ml/½ cup warm water and the olive oil and mix to make a soft, wet dough.

Transfer the dough to a lightly floured surface. Knead, by pushing the dough away from you with the heel of one hand and holding the end nearest you with the other hand so that it stretches out. Fold the dough back over into a ball shape, give it a quarter turn, and stretch it out again. Repeat this process until it is smooth and elastic – about 10 minutes.

Put the dough in a large, lightly oiled bowl. Cover with clingfilm/plastic wrap and leave in a warm place for about 1 hour, or until doubled in size.

Meanwhile, put the baking sheet or pizza stone into the oven and preheat the oven to 230°C (450°F) Gas 8. When the dough has risen, knock it back by flattening it with your fist. Remove from the bowl to a floured surface. Knead again, gradually incorporating the olives and garlic into the dough as you are kneading.

Divide the dough in 2, and roll out each piece on a floured surface to a circle measuring about 30 cm/12 inches diameter. Transfer a lightly floured baking sheet or pizza stone.

Arrange the tomato slices on top of the pizza. Sprinkle with the sugar, salt and pepper and drizzle generously with olive oil. Bake in the preheated oven for about 15–20 minutes or until the pizza is crisp and the tomatoes have begun to caramelize.

Serve each pizza on a plate and finish with the chosen topping.

pizza toppings:
bresaola and parmesan

8 slices bresaola, torn into pieces

55 g/⅔ cup fresh Parmesan cheese shavings (page 11)

55 g/1½ cups rocket/arugula

extra virgin olive oil

freshly ground black pepper

Top each cooked pizza with the bresaola and Parmesan and scatter with rocket/arugula. Sprinkle with oil and black pepper.

mozzarella, pine nuts, capers and basil

175 g/6 oz. mozzarella cheese, preferably buffalo, sliced

55 g/½ cup pine nuts, toasted (page 11)

4 tablespoons baby capers, drained and rinsed

a large handful of basil leaves, torn

extra virgin olive oil

freshly ground black pepper

Tear the slices of mozzarella over each cooked pizza. Sprinkle with the pine nuts and capers, then top with the basil. Sprinkle with oil and black pepper.

feta, onion, parsley and lemon

200 g/1½ cups feta cheese, crumbled into large chunks

½ red onion, finely chopped

a large handful of flat leaf parsley, coarsely chopped

2 tablespoons extra virgin olive oil

1 tablespoon lemon juice

Put all the ingredients in a bowl and mix well. Divide the mixture between the 2 cooked pizzas and serve immediately.

gorgonzola and walnut bread with crunchy celery salad

An easy, yeast-free bread for a beginner baker. For real indulgence, serve with an extra slab of Gorgonzola.

225 g/1½ cups wholemeal/whole-wheat flour

225 g/1½ cups plain/all-purpose flour

1 teaspoon bicarbonate of/baking soda

2 teaspoons cream of tartar

1 teaspoon salt

1 teaspoon (caster) sugar

½ teaspoon cracked black pepper

25 g/2 tablespoons butter, melted

300 ml/1¼ cups milk

175 g/1½ cups roughly crumbled Gorgonzola cheese

85 g/⅔ cup walnut pieces, lightly toasted (page 11)

CELERY SALAD

6 celery stalks, sliced diagonally

1 small red onion, finely chopped

2 tart dessert apples, cored and coarsely chopped

freshly squeezed juice of 1 lemon

2 tablespoons extra virgin olive oil

75 g/2 cups watercress, washed

freshly ground black pepper

a baking sheet, floured

serves 4

Preheat the oven to 190°C (375°F) Gas 5.

Sift the dry ingredients into a large bowl. Put the melted butter and milk into a second bowl and mix.

Make a large well in the centre of the dry ingredients, pour in the butter and milk mixture and, using a wooden spoon, mix to a soft dough. Add the Gorgonzola and walnuts to the dough and knead gently.

Turn out onto a floured surface and shape into a rough oval about 5 cm/2 inches thick. Transfer to a floured baking sheet and, using a sharp knife, make 3 diagonal slashes across the surface of the bread. Dust with a little extra flour and bake in the preheated oven for about 40 minutes until cooked and golden with an evenly crisp base. Transfer to a wire rack and let cool for 20 minutes.

Meanwhile, put the salad ingredients into a large bowl and toss gently. Add black pepper to taste and transfer to a serving bowl. Cut the bread into thick chunks, transfer to a wooden board and serve with the salad.

cherry and cinnamon scones

For light English scones that are nicely risen, handle the dough gently and as little as possible. The mixture needs plenty of air, which is why you sift the dry ingredients.

280 g/1¾ cups plain/all-purpose flour
1 tablespoon baking powder
½ teaspoon salt
1 teaspoon ground cinnamon
55 g/4 tablespoons unsalted butter, diced
25 g/2 tablespoons (caster) sugar
150 ml/⅔ cup milk
1 egg, beaten
175 g/½ cup canned black cherries,
    drained and coarsely chopped
a baking sheet, floured

serves 6

Preheat the oven to 220°C (425°F) Gas 7.

Sift the flour, baking powder, salt and cinnamon into a large bowl and mix. Stir in the diced butter, then using the tips of your fingers, rub in the butter lightly until the mixture looks like coarse breadcrumbs. Add the sugar and stir to mix.

Put the milk and egg into a second bowl and mix. Make a well in the centre of the dry ingredients and pour the milk and egg mixture into the well. Stir in the cherries and, using a round bladed or palette knife, gently bring the mixture together to form a soft dough.

Turn out onto a floured surface and knead very briefly for 30 seconds until just smooth. Do not over-knead or the scones will be tough.

Using your hands, press out to a rough circle, about 2.5 cm/ 1 inch thick. Cut into 6 wedges and transfer to the floured baking sheet.

Dust lightly with flour and bake for 18–20 minutes until risen and golden. Eat hot, or let cool on a wire rack.

TIPS ON BUYING BAKEWARE

• I buy only non-stick bakeware, because it's very user-friendly.

• Treat non-stick bakeware gently – don't scrub or scrape it.

• Buy the best you can afford – the food won't stick to it, and it won't go rusty.

---

crusted lime polenta cake

Fill the cake pan only three-quarters full – the cake will expand as it cooks. Cakes need to cook for longer than scones in a low, gentle oven heat.

225 g/2 sticks unsalted butter
225 g/1 cup (caster) sugar
3 eggs, beaten
½ teaspoon vanilla extract
225 g/2¼ cups ground almonds
grated zest and juice of 3 limes
115 g/¾ cup polenta flour/yellow cornmeal
1 teaspoon baking powder
a pinch of salt

LIME CRUST
juice of 2 limes
3 tablespoons (caster) sugar
mascarpone, or coconut and lime ice cream (page 150), to serve
*a loose-based cake pan, 25 cm/10 inches diameter,
    buttered and floured*

serves 8–10

Preheat the oven to 160°C (325°F) Gas 3. Put the butter and sugar into a large mixing bowl and beat with an electric whisk until pale and light. Gradually add the eggs, whisking all the time. Using a large metal spoon, stir in the vanilla extract and ground almonds, then fold in the lime zest and juice, polenta flour/cornmeal, baking powder and salt.

Spoon into the prepared cake pan and bake for about 1 hour 15 minutes or until just set and golden brown.

Meanwhile, to make the lime crust, put the lime juice and sugar into a bowl and mix well.

When the cake is cooked, prick well with a skewer all over the surface and pour over the lime crust mix. Let cool for 15 minutes in the pan.

Remove from the pan and serve still warm or let cool completely before slicing. Serve with mascarpone or coconut ice cream.

crusted lime polenta cake

the recipes

Now you know the basics, it's time to make use of your new-found skills. Enjoy these fabulous recipes, impress your friends and discover how simple it all is. Don't be afraid of making mistakes – it's all part of the process.

green eggs with salsa verde

eggs

A carton of eggs is the one thing I always have in my fridge. Not only are they the ultimate in fast food, they are also very versatile – eat them hot or cold, on their own, or combined with other foods to make all sorts of sweet or savoury dishes.

green eggs with salsa verde

An omelette-style dish which is fast to cook – have the ingredients ready before you start. To serve more than two people, double the ingredients, but make the eggs in two batches.

4 eggs, preferably organic or free-range
1 teaspoon unsalted butter
50 g/1 cup wild rocket/arugula
salt and freshly ground black pepper

TO SERVE
125 g/2 cups mixed salad leaves
25 g/½ cup walnuts, broken into pieces
fresh Parmesan cheese shavings (page 11)
1 recipe salsa verde (page 143)

serves 2

Crack the eggs into a small bowl and whisk briefly to break up. Add salt and pepper to taste.

Heat the butter in a wok or frying pan until foaming. Add the rocket/arugula and cook, stirring, for about 30 seconds.

Add the eggs and gently swirl around the surface of the wok. Cook until golden brown underneath, but still slightly soft and runny on the top.

Meanwhile, divide the salad between 2 plates and sprinkle with the walnuts. Using 2 wooden spoons, cut the omelette into 4 pieces and put on top of the salad. Top with Parmesan shavings and serve at once with the salsa verde.

quails' eggs with three salts

These are really just tiny hard-boiled eggs, but more fun and unusual than hens' eggs. If you use hens' eggs, increase the cooking time to 6 minutes.

16 quails' eggs
2 teaspoons celery salt

CHILLI/CHILI SALT
1 teaspoon salt
1 teaspoon chilli/chili powder

BLACK PEPPER SALT
1 teaspoon coarse sea salt
1 teaspoon freshly ground black pepper

serves 4

Put the eggs in a saucepan, cover with cold water and bring to the boil. Reduce the heat and simmer for 3 minutes.

Drain and tip the eggs into a bowl of cold water to stop them cooking any further. Let cool in the water, then drain and peel.

To serve, put the quails' eggs in a bowl and the salts in individual small pots. Hand round the eggs and dip into the salt of your choice.

smoked salmon and dill quiche

The secret to good pastry is to have all the ingredients as cold as possible. Baking the pastry case before adding the filling (baking blind) ensures a crisp base. If you don't have a food processor or don't want to make your own pastry, you can buy ready-to-roll fresh or frozen shortcrust pastry dough in supermarkets. If frozen, thaw before rolling out.

PASTRY
280 g/1¾ cups plus 2 tablespoons plain/all-purpose flour
a pinch of salt
140 g/1 stick plus 3 tablespoons chilled butter, diced
2 egg yolks
2 tablespoons very cold water

FILLING
leaves from a bunch of dill, coarsely chopped
2 tablespoons olive oil
1 tablespoon Dijon mustard
325 ml/1¼ cups crème fraîche or sour cream
2 whole eggs, plus 2 egg yolks (below, right)*
175 g/7 oz. smoked salmon
salt and freshly ground black pepper
a loose-based tart pan, 25 cm/10 inches diameter
greaseproof paper and baking beans or uncooked rice

serves 8

Put all the pastry ingredients into a food processor and blend until the ingredients just come together. Don't process beyond this point or the pastry will be tough. Bring the mixture together with your hands and pat into a disc the size of a large plate. Wrap in clingfilm/plastic wrap and refrigerate for 20 minutes. This lets the pastry relax, making it easier to roll out and line the pan. It also prevents the pastry shrinking too much during baking.

Preheat the oven to 200°C (400°F) Gas 6. Put the pastry on a lightly floured surface and roll out a disc to just bigger than the tart pan. Roll the pastry around the rolling pin and drape it over the tart pan. Carefully press the pastry into the pan, making sure there are no air pockets. Cut off excess pastry from the edges. Refrigerate for 15 minutes.

Put the dill, olive oil and mustard in a mini-blender. Process until the mixture comes together, then add salt and pepper.

Line the pastry case with greaseproof paper and fill with baking beans or uncooked rice. Bake in the preheated oven for 10–15 minutes, then remove the paper and beans and return the tart case to the oven for 3–5 minutes until just cooked.

Reduce the oven temperature to 180°C (350°F) Gas 4 while you prepare the filling.

Put the crème fraîche or sour cream in a bowl, add the whole eggs and yolks and beat with a wooden spoon. Add salt and pepper to taste. Spoon the mustard-dill mixture over the base of the tart case. Arrange the smoked salmon on top, then pour in the egg mixture. Bake in the hot oven for 30–35 minutes until just set. Serve hot, warm or cold.

zucchini quiche with sun-dried tomatoes

Follow the pastry recipe for Smoked Salmon and Dill Quiche (left) for this recipe too. When you have made the pastry case, you can try out different fillings, for instance sun-dried peppers in place of the sun-dried tomatoes.

1 prepared baked pastry case (left)
2 tablespoons olive oil
750 g/1½ lbs. courgettes/zucchini, sliced diagonally
325 ml/1¼ cups crème fraîche or sour cream
2 whole eggs, plus 2 egg yolks (below)*
5–6 pieces sun-dried tomatoes in olive oil,
    drained and coarsely chopped
salt and freshly ground black pepper

serves 8

Preheat the oven to 200°C (400°F) Gas 6 and make the pastry as in the previous recipe, so that you have a cooked pastry case ready for the filling.

While the pastry is baking blind, put a few drops of the oil into a frying pan and wipe it over the surface with kitchen paper/paper towels. Heat until hot, add the courgettes/zucchini and fry in batches until golden on both sides.

Reduce the oven temperature to 180°C (350°F) Gas 4 while you prepare the filling.

Put the crème fraîche or sour cream in a bowl, add the whole eggs and yolks and beat with a wooden spoon. Add salt and pepper to taste. Arrange the courgette/zucchini slices in the cooked pastry case, sprinkle with the sun-dried tomatoes, then pour in the egg mixture.

Bake in the preheated oven for about 30–35 minutes until golden and set. Serve hot, warm or cold.

* Don't waste the extra egg whites. Freeze them, then use to make pavlovas (page 146). Defrost completely before beating.

zucchini quiche with sun-dried tomatoes

french toast with smoky bacon and spiked tomatoes

Day-old bread is best for this recipe as it will soak up more of the eggy mixture and fry better than fresh bread. The eggs make the bread puff up inside like a delicious soufflé.

4 eggs

4 slices thick white bread, halved diagonally

12 slices smoked streaky/fatty bacon

2 tablespoons olive oil

4 large plum tomatoes,
    halved lengthways

2 teaspoons sugar

2 teaspoons chilli/chili oil

25 g/2 tablespoons butter

2 tablespoons basil leaves, torn

salt and freshly ground black pepper

serves 4

Preheat the grill/broiler. Put the eggs in a bowl and whisk until mixed. Add plenty of salt and pepper. Pour into a large, shallow dish, then dip the slices of bread in the egg mixture, coating it all over, and set aside for a few minutes to let the egg soak into the bread.

Meanwhile, grill/broil the bacon for 1–2 minutes on each side until crisp. Transfer to a low oven to keep it warm.

Heat 1 tablespoon of the olive oil in a frying pan until hot. Add the tomatoes and sprinkle with the sugar. Fry for 1–2 minutes on each side until caramelized. Sprinkle with the chilli/chili oil and remove from the heat. Transfer to a plate and put into a very low oven to keep warm.

Wipe the frying pan clean with kitchen paper/paper towels, add the butter and remaining oil and heat until hot. Add the egg-soaked bread, in 2 batches if necessary, and fry for 2 minutes on each side until crisp and golden.

Cut the slices of French toast in half diagonally and put 2 triangles on each plate with 3 pieces of bacon on top. Spoon the tomatoes over the bacon, sprinkle with the basil and serve immediately.

parmesan and gruyère soufflés with hot tomato and basil chutney

Don't be afraid of soufflés! They are surprisingly easy to make, and these are part-baked in advance, which takes any timing stresses away. They make great use of eggs – the yolks to set the mixture and whisked whites to give them their light, airy quality. Make sure that everyone is sitting down ready to eat when the soufflés come out of the oven – you have to serve them straightaway.

300 ml/1¼ cups milk
1 slice of onion
a pinch of freshly grated nutmeg
1 bay leaf
45 g/4 tablespoons butter
45 g/⅓ cup plain/all-purpose flour
1 teaspoon wholegrain mustard
50 g/½ cup grated Gruyère cheese
50 g/½ cup grated Parmesan cheese
3 large eggs, separated (page 110)
200 ml/¾ cup double/heavy cream
salt and freshly ground black pepper
a handful of rocket/arugula leaves, to serve

HOT TOMATO AND BASIL CHUTNEY
1 tablespoon extra virgin olive oil
1 large shallot, finely chopped
250 g/8 oz. baby plum tomatoes, halved
a pinch of brown sugar
2 tablespoons balsamic vinegar
a squeeze of fresh lemon juice
2 tablespoons torn basil leaves
salt and freshly ground black pepper
6 ramekins, 150 ml/⅔ cup each, well buttered

serves 6

To make the chutney, heat the oil in a saucepan. Add the shallot and cook over medium heat for 2–3 minutes. Add the tomatoes, sugar and vinegar and cook for 5–6 minutes, until the tomatoes just begin to soften. Add the lemon juice and plenty of salt and pepper. Stir in the basil.

Put the milk, onion, nutmeg and bay leaf into a saucepan and heat gently until just boiling. Remove the pan from the heat and set aside to infuse for 30 minutes. Remove and discard the onion and bay leaf. Preheat the oven to 180°C (350°F) Gas 4.

Melt the butter in a second saucepan. Add the flour and cook gently, stirring, for 30 seconds. Remove the pan from the heat and gradually add the milk, whisking all the time, until you have a smooth sauce. Return the pan to the heat and stir until the sauce boils and thickens.

Remove the pan from the heat and stir in the mustard, three-quarters of the Gruyère and Parmesan, then the egg yolks. Add salt and pepper to taste.

Put the egg whites in a large, clean bowl and whisk with a metal whisk until stiff. Using a large metal spoon, carefully fold the whites into the cheese mixture until no flecks of white are showing. Pour into the ramekins to two-thirds full.

Put the ramekins in a roasting pan and pour boiling water into the pan to come halfway up the ramekins. This provides a gentle, even heat which stops the eggs separating as they cook. Bake in the preheated oven for 15–20 minutes until set. Remove the ramekins from the pan and set aside to cool.

Before serving, preheat the oven to 220°C (425°F) Gas 7. Loosen the soufflé edges with a knife and turn them out into a shallow ovenproof dish. Sprinkle with the remaining Gruyère and Parmesan and pour over the cream.

Transfer to the oven for about 10–12 minutes, until puffed and golden. Serve at once with a few rocket/arugula leaves and a spoonful of hot tomato and basil chutney.

salami and thyme popovers

Egg-based batters can be made savoury or sweet. These popovers are savoury, the clafoutis and frittata (right) are both sweet. The popovers are an updated version of the British classic, toad-in-the-hole – the egg yolks add richness to the batter, while the whites make the cooked popovers light and puffy. Serve them as an accompaniment to other dishes, such as roasted meats or other main courses, or the other dishes listed below. You can also serve them as a starter, with a crisp salad and tomato chutney.

115 g/¾ cup plain/all-purpose flour
a good pinch of salt
2 eggs
300 ml/1¼ cups milk
8 teaspoons olive oil
4 tablespoons thyme leaves
115 g/4 oz. salami, skinned and chopped
    into 1-cm/½-inch cubes
freshly ground black pepper
12-hole muffin pan

serves 4

Preheat the oven to 220°C (425°F) Gas 7.

Sift the flour and salt into a large bowl. Make a well in the centre and crack the eggs into the well. Using a wooden spoon, gradually mix the eggs into the flour. Using a metal whisk, slowly whisk in the milk, until you have a smooth batter. Cover and refrigerate for 30 minutes.

SEPARATING EGGS

Have 2 bowls ready. Tap the egg on the side of one bowl to crack it in the middle. Using your thumbs, pull open the two halves with the cracked side facing upwards, tipping the yolk into one half and letting any white fall into the bowl. Tip the yolk back and forth between the 2 shell halves until there is no white left around the yolk. Tip the yolk into the other bowl. If any yolk slips into the white, use a shell to scoop it out.

Put 1 teaspoon olive oil into 8 of the muffin holes and put in the hot oven until smoking hot. Add plenty of black pepper to the batter and stir in the thyme. Pour the batter into the 8 hot muffin holes and sprinkle with the salami. Return them to the oven for about 20–25 minutes until risen and golden.

Serve either with bean, bacon and rosemary ragout (page 90) or spinach and green bean salad (page 126).

plum clafoutis

These baby versions of the popular French dessert are made with sweet egg batter. Clafoutis is usually made with cherries, which you can also use in this recipe in place of plums – apricots, nectarines, blueberries or blackcurrants are good substitutes too. If you have any leftover batter, refrigerate for up to one day and use for pancakes.

115 g/¾ cup plain/all-purpose flour
a good pinch of salt
55 g/¼ cup (caster) sugar
2 eggs
300 ml/1¼ cups milk
1 teaspoon vanilla extract
8 teaspoons sunflower oil
4 plums, halved and pitted

TO SERVE
icing/confectioners' sugar
extra thick double/heavy cream
12-hole muffin pan

makes 8

Preheat the oven to 220°C (425°F) Gas 7.

Sift the flour and salt into a large bowl and stir in the sugar. Make a well in the centre and crack the eggs into the well. Using a wooden spoon, gradually mix the eggs into the flour. Using a metal whisk, slowly whisk in the milk, until you have a smooth batter. Stir in the vanilla extract. Cover and refrigerate for 30 minutes.

Put 1 teaspoon sunflower oil into 8 of the holes in the muffin pan and put into the preheated oven until smoking hot. Pour the batter into the 8 muffin holes until half full, then put one plum half, skin side up, in each hole.

Return them to the oven for 20–25 minutes until risen and golden. Dust with icing/confectioners' sugar and serve with cream.

sweet blueberry and cinnamon frittata with maple syrup

This dish is a cross between a soufflé and an omelette – two of the great egg dishes. It starts on top of the stove like an omelette and is finished in the oven like a soufflé. Make sure you use a pan with an ovenproof handle so it's suitable for both. You need good-quality (and therefore more expensive) maple syrup for this recipe.

4 eggs, separated (below, left)
2 teaspoons ground cinnamon
50 g/¼ cup (caster) sugar
150 g/⅔ cup mascarpone cheese
25 g/2 tablespoons unsalted butter
250 g/2 cups blueberries

sweet blueberry and cinnamon
frittata with maple syrup

TO SERVE
vanilla ice cream
3 tablespoons good-quality maple syrup
non-stick ovenproof frying pan,
    30 cm/12 inches diameter

serves 6

Preheat the oven to 190°C (380°F)
Gas 5. Put the egg yolks, cinnamon and
half the sugar into a large bowl. Using
an electric whisk, beat the mixture until

pale and creamy. Add the mascarpone
and whisk for 1 minute until smooth.

Remove the beaters from the whisk and
wash and dry them. Put the egg whites
into a large, clean bowl and whisk until
stiff. Add the remaining sugar and beat
for a further 2 minutes until stiff and
shiny. Using a large metal spoon, fold
1 spoonful of the egg whites into the egg
and mascarpone mixture. Gently fold in
the remaining egg whites.

Heat the butter in the frying pan until
foaming. Add the egg mixture and cook
over a medium heat for 1 minute.

Dot the blueberries over the top,
transfer to the preheated oven and bake
for about 25 minutes until golden and
just set. Serve with ice cream and
maple syrup.

tomato tapenade salad

salads

This chapter is called salads, but salads aren't just lettuce. You can make them with lots of other things and serve them at any time of day – even as a meal on their own.

tomato tapenade salad

In Provence, a tapenade is a paste of anchovies, capers and olives, but I've used just capers and olives as the basis for the salad. Use the ripest red tomatoes, so there are plenty of lovely juices to soak up with the toasted focaccia.

1 small focaccia bread, torn into bite-sized pieces
8 large tomatoes, each chopped into 8 pieces
20 kalamata olives, squashed and pitted
2 tablespoons baby capers, rinsed and drained
1 garlic clove, chopped
2 tablespoons extra virgin olive oil
½ teaspoon salt
a pinch of sugar
freshly ground black pepper

TO SERVE
a bunch of basil leaves, torn
extra virgin olive oil
a baking sheet

serves 4

Preheat the oven to 220°C (425°F) Gas 7. Put the focaccia pieces onto a baking sheet. Put in the preheated oven and bake for 12–15 minutes until golden.

Meanwhile, put the tomatoes into a large bowl. Add the olives, capers, garlic, oil, salt, sugar and black pepper.

Divide the toasted focaccia pieces between 4 large serving plates and top with a large spoonful of the tomato mixture. Sprinkle with basil and oil, then serve.

hot crunchy croutons with smoked bacon and avocado

One of my all-time favourite warm salads. Don't slice the avocado until the last minute, so that it doesn't discolour – you can do this while the croutons are cooking in the oven.

125 g/4 oz. pancetta or bacon, cut into 2-cm/1-inch pieces
1 tablespoon olive oil
3 thick slices rustic-style bread, cut into bite-sized pieces
1 cos/romaine lettuce, washed, dried and torn into large pieces
1 butterhead lettuce, washed, dried and torn into large pieces
1 recipe dijon dressing (page 145)
2 ripe Hass avocados, halved, pitted, peeled and thickly
   sliced diagonally
freshly ground black pepper
a large, non-stick baking sheet

serves 4

Preheat the oven to 200°C (400°F) Gas 6. Put the pancetta or bacon on the baking sheet, put into the oven and bake for 5 minutes.

Add the oil and bread and turn it with a spoon to coat the bread. Sprinkle with pepper. Return to the oven and bake for a further 20–25 minutes, moving the bread around the sheet with a large spoon a few times during cooking to stop it sticking, until the bread is golden and the bacon is crisp.

Put the lettuce into a large salad bowl, add the dressing and toss gently. Put the avocado, hot bacon and croutons over the salad, toss again and serve immediately.

peppered goat cheese

Cheese, especially blue, goat milk or creamy, make easy, excellent salads. Gentle cooking gives this one extra pizzazz (you need cheese with a rind if you're going to cook it). Serve it as a starter or for lunch.

1 tablespoon freshly ground black pepper
2 goat cheeses, 100 g/4 oz. each, with rind, halved
    crossways
2 large handfuls of wild rocket/arugula
2 large handfuls of baby leaf spinach
1 tablespoon extra virgin olive oil
juice of ½ lemon
salt
chilli/chili oil, to serve (optional)

serves 4

Sprinkle the black pepper onto a plate and lightly press both sides of each cheese half into the pepper to coat.

Heat a stove-top grill pan until hot. Add the peppered cheese slices, cut side down, and cook for 2 minutes. Turn them over, cover loosely with foil and cook for a further 4–5 minutes until the cheese is soft but not completely melted.

Meanwhile, put the rocket/arugula, spinach, oil and lemon juice into a large bowl. Add salt to taste and toss to coat.

Divide the salad between 4 large serving plates or flat bowls and top with a slice of peppered cheese. Sprinkle with chilli/chili oil, if using, and serve.

seared peppered beef salad with horseradish dressing

A summery way of enjoying roast beef without too much heat from the kitchen. Par-boiling the accompanying potatoes before roasting means that they won't dry out and shrivel as they roast (see pages 15 and 79 for cooking tips).

500 g/1 lb. baby new potatoes, unpeeled, par-boiled for 12–15 minutes
    (page 15), until nearly cooked through
2 tablespoons olive oil
250 g/8 oz. baby plum tomatoes
4 fillet steaks, 125 g/4 oz. each
1 tablespoon Worcestershire sauce
100 g/2 cups wild rocket/arugula
125 g/1 cup sugar snap peas, trimmed, blanched, refreshed (page 15)
    and halved lengthways
salt and freshly ground black pepper

HORSERADISH DRESSING
3 tablespoons crème fraîche or sour cream
1–2 tablespoons creamed horseradish
a squeeze of fresh lemon juice

serves 4

Preheat the oven to 220°C (425°F) Gas 7.

Put the par-boiled potatoes in a roasting pan and toss with 1 tablespoon oil, to coat. Sprinkle with salt and black pepper, transfer to the preheated oven and roast for 25–30 minutes until browned and starting to crisp.

Remove from the oven and, using a large metal spoon, push the potatoes to one end of the pan, in a pile. Put the baby plum tomatoes into the empty half of the pan and sprinkle with 1 tablespoon olive oil, salt and pepper. Roast in the oven for 15 minutes until just soft.

Meanwhile, put all the dressing ingredients into a bowl and mix. Add salt and pepper to taste.

Sprinkle the steaks with plenty of black pepper and drizzle with the Worcestershire sauce. Preheat a stove-top grill pan, add the beef and sear for 1–2 minutes on each side or until cooked to your liking. Set aside to rest.

Put the rocket/arugula and the sugar snap peas into a bowl and toss well. Divide between 4 serving plates. Spoon the potatoes and tomatoes around the rocket/arugula and peas.

Slice the beef fillet diagonally and arrange the slices over the salad. Top with a dollop of horseradish dressing and serve, with any remaining sauce served separately.

seared peppered beef salad
with horseradish dressing

bitter leaves
with walnut dressing

bitter leaves with walnut dressing

The secret of this salad is to have the walnuts sizzling hot. Get the salad ready and add the walnuts as soon as they come out of the oven. Walnut oil is great in dressings, but just use extra olive oil if you can't find it. Keep nuts and nut oils (except peanut oil) in the refrigerator, because they can go rancid quickly.

100 g/1 cup walnuts

1 teaspoon walnut oil

1 teaspoon salt

1 head of radicchio, leaves separated, washed and dried

2 heads of chicory/Belgian endive, leaves separated, washed and dried

1 small curly endive lettuce, leaves separated, washed and dried

WALNUT DRESSING

1 tablespoon walnut oil

1 tablespoon extra virgin olive oil

a good squeeze of fresh lemon juice

freshly ground black pepper

serves 4

Preheat the oven to 200°C (400°F) Gas 6.

Put the walnuts, walnut oil and salt in a small bowl and stir. Transfer to a baking sheet in a single layer and cook in the oven for 8–10 minutes until toasted all over.

Meanwhile, put the salad leaves into a large salad bowl. Put all the dressing ingredients into a separate bowl and whisk well. Add freshly ground black pepper to taste.

WASHING AND DRYING SALAD LEAVES

• Wash crisp-leafed lettuces and other salad leaves in a bowl of water, transfer to a salad spinner and spin dry. Wrap, put in a cloth or kitchen paper/paper towels and store in the refrigerator – the leaves will become even crisper.

• Rinse soft-leafed greens such as lamb's lettuce/corn salad or rocket/arugula just before using and let drain in a colander. Pat dry with kitchen paper/paper towels and serve as soon as possible.

• If you haven't got a salad spinner, wash the leaves, then pat dry with kitchen paper/paper towels.

To serve, sprinkle the hot walnuts over the salad leaves, pour over the dressing and toss well. Serve immediately as a salad or with crusty bread and shavings of Parmesan (page 11) as a lunch or salad starter/appetizer.

tuna carpaccio salad

Carpaccio is usually raw beef, but this recipe uses lightly seared tuna instead. As it will be served very rare, make sure the tuna you buy is really fresh – and remember that it carries on cooking after you take it out of the pan.

3 tablespoons teriyaki sauce

1 teaspoon (runny) honey

juice of 2 limes

4 tablespoons peanut oil

2 very fresh thick tuna steaks

freshly ground black pepper

SALAD

175 g/⅓ cup beansprouts

6 radishes, thinly sliced

1 tablespoon toasted sesame seeds (page 11)

a large bunch of coriander/cilantro

2.5-cm/1-inch piece of fresh ginger, peeled and finely chopped

salt and freshly ground black pepper

1 lime, cut into wedges, to serve

serves 4

To make the marinade, put the teriyaki sauce, honey, lime juice and 1 tablespoon peanut oil in a bowl and whisk well. Add black pepper to taste. Remove 3 tablespoons of the marinade and reserve. Add the tuna to the remaining marinade, cover and refrigerate for up to 2 hours.

When ready to serve, put the beansprouts, radishes, sesame seeds and coriander/cilantro in a large bowl and toss gently. Add plenty of salt and black pepper. Put the ginger, reserved marinade and remaining oil in a bowl. Whisk well.

Heat a large, dry frying pan until very hot. Add the tuna, sear for 1 minute on each side, then remove from the pan to a board. Let rest for 2 minutes and, using a very sharp knife, cut the tuna into thin slices, about 1 cm/½ inch thick. Divide the slices between 4 serving plates, covering the whole surface of the plate in a single, overlapping layer.

Put a handful of the beansprout salad in the centre of each plate and drizzle with the dressing. Serve with the lime wedges.

soups

I'm a big fan of one-pot meals, so I love soups. Smooth and elegant or chunky and hearty – homemade soup is hard to beat and is incredibly quick to make.

wild mushroom soup with sour cream and chives

Dried porcini have a gorgeous, intense taste and you only need to add a few to fresh mushrooms to produce a lovely, rich soup. Always rinse porcini well, to remove dust or grit.

10 g/1 oz. dried porcini mushrooms, rinsed thoroughly
50 g/4 tablespoons butter
500 g/1 lb. large open mushrooms, sliced
2 garlic cloves, crushed
2 slices of white bread, crusts removed
150 ml/⅔ cup sour cream
a small bunch of chives, chopped
salt and freshly ground black pepper

serves 4

Put the porcini in a small bowl. Cover with 750 ml/3 cups boiling water and let soak for 30 minutes.

Meanwhile, put the butter into a large saucepan or non-stick wok and heat until melted. Add the sliced mushrooms and cook for about 5 minutes until soft.

Drain the porcini, reserving the soaking liquid. Coarsely chop, then add to the mushrooms in the pan. Cook for a further 2 minutes, then add the garlic.

Tear the bread into the pan. Add the reserved porcini soaking liquid and salt and pepper to taste. Bring to the boil, reduce the heat and simmer for 10 minutes.

Transfer the soup to a food processor or blender and process until almost smooth. Ladle into bowls and top with a spoonful of sour cream. Sprinkle with chives and freshly ground black pepper, then serve.

green minestrone

Moving away from the traditional tomato and meat flavour, this vibrant soup is spring and summer in a bowl.

2 tablespoons olive oil
2 leeks, washed and finely sliced
150 ml/⅔ cup white wine
1.5 litres/6 cups vegetable stock
125 g/4 oz. spaghetti, broken into 5-cm/2-inch pieces
125 g/4 oz. baby asparagus, halved
125 g/4 oz. fine green beans, trimmed and halved
125 g/1 cup frozen peas, preferably petits pois
2 courgettes/zucchini, trimmed and cut into 5-mm/¼-inch dice
leaves from a large bunch of basil, torn
salt and freshly ground black pepper

TO SERVE
fresh Parmesan cheese shavings (page 11)
extra virgin olive oil

serves 4

Heat the oil in a large saucepan or non-stick wok. Add the leeks and fry gently for about 10 minutes, until softened but not golden. Pour in the wine and stock, add salt and pepper to taste and bring to the boil. Add the spaghetti and simmer for 8 minutes.

Add the asparagus and beans and cook for 1 minute. Add the peas and courgettes/zucchini, return to the boil and simmer for 2 minutes. Add the basil and salt and pepper to taste.

Ladle the minestrone into 4 deep plates or bowls. Sprinkle with the Parmesan shavings and oil. Add plenty of freshly ground black pepper and serve.

miso chicken broth
with noodles

Put the chicken, shoyu and ginger in a bowl and set aside to marinate.

Cook the noodles in a saucepan of boiling water for 10–12 minutes for udon or 4–5 minutes for egg noodles, until tender, or follow the manufacturer's instructions. Drain.

Add the chicken and its marinade to the broth and simmer gently for 1–2 minutes. Add the spinach and simmer for a further 1 minute.

Divide the noodles between 4 deep bowls and pour the broth over the top.

Sprinkle with the spring onions/scallions and furikake seasoning and serve at once.

watercress and bacon chowder

Chowder is a hearty soup, originally from New England and often made with seafood, especially clams. This version is free of seafood, but it still has all the robust goodness of a classic chowder.

25 g/2 tablespoons unsalted butter
125 g/4 oz. (rindless smoked) bacon, chopped into
  2.5-cm/1-inch pieces
1 large onion, finely chopped
1 tablespoon plain/all-purpose flour
375 ml/1½ cups milk
500 ml/2 cups chicken stock
250 g/8 oz. new potatoes, quartered lengthways
leaves from a bunch of watercress, chopped
freshly ground black pepper

serves 4

Put the butter into a large saucepan or wok and heat until melted. Add the bacon and cook over medium heat for 4–5 minutes until golden.

Add the onion and cook gently over low heat for about 10 minutes until softened and translucent. Add the flour and cook, stirring with a wooden spoon, for about 1 minute. Gradually add the milk and stock and bring to the boil, stirring constantly.

Add the potatoes and simmer for 10–12 minutes until tender when pierced with a knife. Stir in the watercress and sprinkle generously with pepper.

Ladle into soup bowls and serve.

miso chicken broth with noodles

Furikake is a Japanese seasoning made from sesame seeds and dried seaweed. You can buy it in most big supermarkets, but if you can't find it, use toasted sesame seeds instead.

300 g/10 oz. boneless, skinless chicken breast, thinly sliced
2 tablespoons shoyu (Japanese soy sauce) or soy sauce
2.5-cm/1-inch piece of fresh ginger, peeled and finely chopped
400 g/14 oz. dried udon or egg noodles
125 g/1 cup baby leaf spinach
2 spring onions/scallions, finely sliced diagonally
4 teaspoons furikake seasoning

CHICKEN BROTH
900 ml/4 cups fresh chicken stock
1 sachet instant miso soup
4 tablespoons shoyu or soy sauce
2 garlic cloves, sliced
1 teaspoon sugar
125 g/1 cup shiitake mushrooms, stalks removed and discarded,
  caps thickly sliced

serves 4

Put all the broth ingredients into a saucepan. Add 300 ml/ 1¼ cups cold water and bring to the boil. Reduce the heat and simmer for 15–20 minutes.

rich red pepper
and bean soup

Canned beans can form the basis of lots of filling,
easy-to-make soups, salads and main courses/entrées,
so keep several cans of each kind in your storecupboard.

2 large red (bell) peppers, halved, seeded and cut
   into 1-cm/½-inch slices
3 tablespoons olive oil
1 large onion, finely chopped
150 ml/⅔ cup dry white wine
820 g/1½ lbs. canned butter/lima beans, drained and rinsed
700 ml/3 cups vegetable stock
125 g/4 oz. fine green beans
salt and freshly ground black pepper
chilli/chili or garlic oil, to serve

serves 4

Preheat the oven to 200°C (400°F) Gas 6. Put the (bell)
peppers in a roasting pan, drizzle with 1 tablespoon olive oil
and sprinkle with salt and pepper. Transfer to the preheated
oven and roast for 30 minutes.

Heat the remaining oil in a large saucepan. Add the onion
and cook over medium heat for 10 minutes, or until softened
and translucent.

Add the wine to the onion and boil for 1 minute. Add the
butter/lima beans and stock and black pepper to taste. Bring
to the boil, reduce the heat and simmer for 15 minutes.

Meanwhile, add the green beans to the (bell) peppers in the
oven and roast for a further 8–10 minutes.

Transfer the butter/lima-bean mixture to a food processor
or blender and blend until smooth. Ladle into soup plates or
bowls, then top with a spoonful of the (bell) peppers and
beans. Drizzle with the chilli/chili or garlic oil and serve.

mediterranean fish stew

fish and seafood

There are so many varieties of wonderful fish and seafood – make the most of them! For maximum flavour and freshness, buy from your fishmonger or local fish counter and cook it the same day.

mediterranean fish stew

Prawn/shrimp shells are full of flavour, which seeps into the sauce and contributes to its richness. Eat this dish with your fingers and mop up with plenty of crusty fresh bread.

1 large fennel bulb, with leafy tops
2 tablespoons olive oil
2 garlic cloves, crushed
200 ml/¾ cup dry white wine
300 ml/1¼ cups fish stock
800 g/4 cups canned chopped tomatoes
a pinch of sugar
250 g/1 cup cherry tomatoes, halved
500 g/1 lb. monkfish fillet, cut into 4-cm/1¼-inch chunks
12 mussels, scrubbed and beards removed (page 32)
12 large, unpeeled, uncooked prawns/shrimp, heads removed
salt and freshly ground black pepper

TO SERVE
extra virgin olive oil
pimento paste (page 144) (optional)

serves 4

Remove the leafy tops from the fennel bulb, chop them coarsely and set aside. Cut the bulb into quarters, remove and discard the core, then finely chop the bulb.

Heat the oil in a large saucepan or wok. Add the fennel bulb and fry for 5 minutes. Add the garlic and fry for a further 1 minute. Add the wine, stock, canned tomatoes and sugar and stir well. Bring to the boil, reduce the heat then simmer for 5 minutes. Add the cherry tomatoes and cook for a further 5 minutes. Add plenty of salt and freshly ground black pepper.

Add the monkfish and return to simmering. Stir in the mussels and prawns/shrimp, cover and cook for about 5 minutes, or until the mussels have opened and the fish is cooked.

Ladle the stew into deep plates or bowls and spoon the pimento paste, if using, on top. Sprinkle with the fennel tops and olive oil and serve.

Variation Though not authentically Mediterranean, salmon is also delicious in this stew. Clams are good too, but can be sandy, so cook them in a separate saucepan and strain the liquid before adding them to the stew.

PREPARING SEAFOOD

• If using larger prawns/shrimp, cut them down the back and pull out and discard the black thread. If the prawns/shrimp are small, don't bother.
• Squid can be fiddly to clean yourself – get the fishmonger or fish counter to do it for you, or buy it ready-cleaned from the supermarket.
• Scrub mussels and pull off the seaweedy "beards". Tap them against the kitchen bench – if they don't close, throw them away. After they're cooked, throw away any that haven't opened.

4 baby bok choy, blanched and refreshed (page 15)
2 tablespoons toasted sesame seeds (page 11)
freshly ground black pepper

DRESSING
4 tablespoons sunflower/safflower oil
a bunch of spring onions/scallions, cut into strips
3 tablespoons light soy sauce
freshly squeezed juice of 1 large orange
5-cm/2-inch piece of fresh ginger, peeled and grated
1 large garlic clove, crushed
2 teaspoons sesame oil
salt and freshly ground black pepper

serves 4

Put the lime juice, olive oil and teriyaki sauce in a bowl and mix well. Put the tuna steaks in a shallow dish and pour over the teriyaki mixture. Sprinkle with black pepper, turn to coat and set aside for 30 minutes.

Meanwhile, to make the dressing, put 1 tablespoon of the sunflower/safflower oil in a frying pan and heat until hot. Add the spring onions and stir-fry for 30 seconds. Remove from the heat and stir in the remaining dressing ingredients. Add salt and pepper to taste.

Put the noodles, sugar snap peas, carrots and tomatoes into a mixing bowl. Add the warm dressing and toss gently until all the ingredients are well coated.

Heat a stove-top grill pan or frying pan until hot. Add the tuna steaks and sear for 1–2 minutes on each side. Remove from the pan and cut the steaks into slices. Pile a little of the noodle salad and bok choy onto each serving plate and sprinkle with the sesame seeds. Top with the seared tuna slices and serve at once.

californian tuna noodle salad

A light, aromatic dish. Be careful not to overcook the tuna – it should be rare – and don't forget that it will go on cooking even after you take it off the heat. The green vegetables are blanched and refreshed, as described on page 15, for best colour and texture.

juice of 1 lime
2 tablespoons olive oil
2 tablespoons teriyaki sauce
4 tuna steaks, 150 g/6 oz. each
200 g/8 oz. fine egg noodles, cooked and drained (page 21)
125 g/1½ cups sugar snap peas, blanched, refreshed (page 15)
    and halved lengthways
2 large carrots, finely cut into matchstick strips
4 baby plum tomatoes, halved

COOKING FISH

• It's important not to overcook fish – cook it just until it is opaque all the way through.
• Remember it keeps cooking after you remove it from the pan.
• Tuna can be underdone (pink in the middle), but it must be very fresh. To make sure, buy it from a fishmonger or fish counter.

marinated vodka salmon

This is salmon served ceviche-style – a method in which fish or seafood is "cooked" by the citrus juice in its marinade. It is a popular way to eat seafood in Central and South America. Fresh fish is absolutely essential.

375 g/14 oz. salmon fillet
4 spring onions/scallions, finely sliced diagonally
1 red chilli/chile, seeded and finely chopped (page 43)
3 tablespoons vodka
juice of 2 limes
2 tablespoons extra virgin olive oil
leaves from a bunch of coriander/cilantro
salt and freshly ground black pepper
black rye bread, to serve

serves 4

Put the salmon fillet on a board and cut it crossways into 1-cm/½-inch slices. Arrange the salmon slices in overlapping layers on a large serving plate. Sprinkle with salt and freshly ground black pepper.

Put the spring onions/scallions, chilli, vodka and lime juice in a small bowl and mix well. Pour the mixture over the salmon and set aside for 30 minutes, to let the salmon "cook".

Sprinkle with salt and pepper and drizzle with the olive oil. Top with the coriander/cilantro and serve with black rye bread.

trout fishcakes

I favour trout over salmon for making fishcakes, as it is moist and has a lovely, earthy flavour. The shaped cakes need to be chilled so they will keep their shape when fried.

500 g/1 lb. potatoes, cut into small chunks
½ teaspoon salt
500 g/1 lb. rainbow trout fillets
250 ml/1 cup milk
25 g/2 tablespoons butter
a small bunch of flat leaf parsley, chopped
a small bunch of chives, chopped
flour, for shaping the fishcakes
1 egg, beaten
125 g/2½ cups fresh white breadcrumbs
sunflower oil, for frying
125 g/4 oz. fine green beans, blanched and
    refreshed (page 15)
125 g/1 cup baby spinach leaves
salt and freshly ground black pepper

TO SERVE (optional)
extra chives
tartare sauce
quick aïoli (page 144)
lemon beurre blanc (page 145)
dijon dressing (page 145)

serves 4

Put the potatoes in a saucepan, cover with water and bring to the boil. Add the salt and simmer gently for 15 minutes, until the potatoes are tender.

Meanwhile, put the fish in a large, shallow saucepan and pour over the milk. Cover, bring to the boil, reduce the heat and simmer very gently for 5–6 minutes, until the fish is opaque all the way through and just cooked. Using a slotted spoon, remove to a plate and let cool. Remove and discard the skin, then coarsely flake the fish.

Drain the potatoes and return them to the pan. Add the butter and mash until smooth. Put into a large bowl, add the parsley and chives and mix. Add plenty of salt and black pepper. Using a large metal spoon, gently fold in the flaked fish.

Using floured hands, shape the mixture into 4 round cakes, about 2.5 cm/1 inch thick. Dip them first into the beaten egg and then into the breadcrumbs to coat all over. Refrigerate for 30 minutes.

Put 2 cm/¾ inch oil into a large frying pan and heat until hot. Add the fishcakes and fry over a medium heat for 3–4 minutes on each side, until golden brown and heated through.

Toss the beans and spinach together in a bowl, divide between 4 plates and put a fishcake on top. Serve with extra chives and one of the sauces.

FRYING FISHCAKES

Put enough oil in the pan for the food to cook evenly on both sides, allowing for some of the fat to be absorbed. This will avoid a "tide mark" on the fishcakes. The level should be more than halfway up the sides of the fishcakes.

chicken and duck

Chicken is a great favourite in our house and we are always revisiting old favourites as well as trying new ideas. Duck is popular too – don't save it for special occasions.

mexican chicken burgers

Chicken thighs have more flavour and are less dry than breast, so are ideal for these spicy burgers. Shape the burgers with wet hands, to stop the mixture sticking to them.

1 tablespoon olive oil, plus extra for brushing

1 small red onion, finely chopped

1 large garlic clove, crushed

2 teaspoons ground coriander

250 g/8 oz. boneless, skinless chicken thighs, each cut into 6

50 g/1 cup breadcrumbs

15 g/½ oz. bottled/canned jalapeño chillies/chiles, drained and rinsed

1 egg, beaten

salt and freshly ground black pepper

TO SERVE

4 small wholemeal/whole-wheat hamburger buns, halved crossways

salad leaves

chunky guacamole (page 143)

1 lime, cut into wedges

serves 4

Heat the oil in a small saucepan. Add the onion and fry for 5 minutes until softened. Add the garlic and ground coriander and cook for a further 1 minute. Let cool.

Transfer to a food processor and add the chicken, breadcrumbs, chillies/chiles, egg and some salt and pepper. Blend until you get a coarse paste.

Transfer the mixture from the food processor to a clean work surface. Using wet hands, shape the mixture into 4 burgers and refrigerate for 30 minutes.

Heat a stove-top grill pan until hot, brush with a little oil, add the burgers and fry gently for 6–7 minutes on each side until thoroughly cooked through.

Put each burger in a hamburger bun with salad and chunky guacamole and serve with lime wedges.

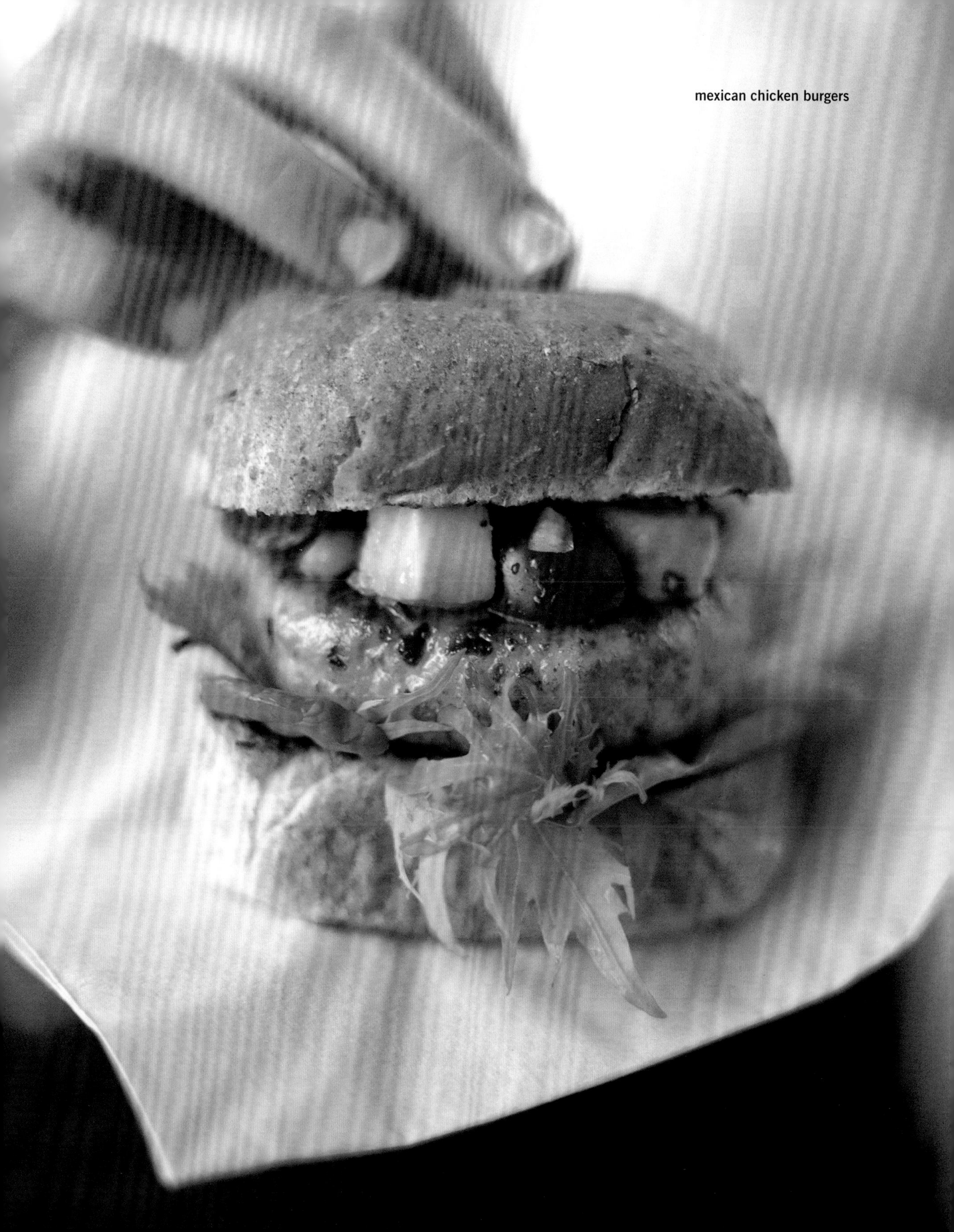

mexican chicken burgers

coq au vin

This modern version of the classic dish of chicken cooked in wine is a handy shortcut. Cutting slashes in the chicken lets the marinade soak into and flavour the meat, while keeping it tender and moist.

4 boneless, skinless chicken breasts
150 ml/⅔ cup red wine
1 garlic clove, sliced
2 tablespoons olive oil
a sprig of thyme

SAUCE
20 g/1 oz. dried porcini mushrooms, rinsed thoroughly
1 tablespoon olive oil
6 shallots, halved
a pinch of sugar
125 g/4 oz. (smoked) bacon, chopped
1 garlic clove, crushed
2 teaspoons plain/all-purpose flour
150 ml/⅔ cup red wine
150 ml/⅔ cup port
a sprig of thyme, plus 4 sprigs to serve
salt and freshly ground black pepper

serves 4

Using a small, sharp knife, slash the top of each chicken breast in a criss-cross fashion, taking care not to cut all the way through. Put the breasts in a shallow dish. Add the red wine, garlic, oil and thyme and mix. Cover and refrigerate for 20 minutes. The chicken will absorb most of the marinade.

Meanwhile, to make the sauce, put the dried porcini in a bowl and cover with 150 ml/⅔ cup boiling water. Let soak for 15 minutes, then drain, reserving the liquid. (The liquid can sometimes be gritty, so strain it through a tea strainer.) Coarsely chop the mushrooms.

Heat the oil in a frying pan. Add the shallots and sugar and fry for 10 minutes until golden. Add the bacon and garlic and fry for a further 5 minutes. Stir in the flour and cook for 1 minute. Add the mushrooms and their soaking liquid, red wine, port and a sprig of thyme. Bring to the boil, reduce the heat and simmer for 20 minutes until syrupy. Add salt and pepper to taste.

Meanwhile, heat a stove-top grill pan until hot. Transfer the chicken to the grill pan, discarding any remaining marinade. Cook for about 5 minutes on each side, until the chicken is cooked through, with no trace of pink in the middle. Serve with the sauce poured over, topped with a sprig of thyme.

CHICKEN COOKING TIPS

• It's important to cook chicken all the way through. To test, push a skewer or small sharp knife into the thickest part – this is normally the drumstick or thigh. The juices that run out should be clear or golden – if they are pink or bloody, you must cook it for longer.
• To check whether chicken breasts are cooked, cut one to see. Cut through the thickest part – it should be opaque all the way through, with no trace of blood.
• Boneless, skinless chicken is quick and easy to cook, but if you cook it with the skin on and the bone in, it will have more flavour. Skin keeps it moist, while the bone helps conduct heat.

honeyed duck with mango salsa

honeyed duck with mango salsa

Duck always works well with fruit and this recipe is also good with nectarines. Pricking the duck skin stops it shrinking as it cooks, while the honey-soy mixture produces a delicious, crackly skin.

4 small to medium duck breasts, skin on
1 tablespoon soy sauce
1 tablespoon honey
salt

MANGO SALSA
1 large, ripe mango
1 orange (bell) pepper, halved, seeded and diced
6 spring onions/scallions, finely sliced
2 tablespoons olive oil
grated zest and juice of 1 orange
juice of 1 lime
4 sprigs of coriander/cilantro

serves 4

Cut the sides off the mango in 4 slabs, from top to bottom, and discard the stone/seed and surrounding flesh. With a small, sharp knife, cut a criss-cross pattern into the flesh of each piece, down to the skin. Push the skin with your thumbs to invert and scrape off the cubes of flesh with a knife.

Put the mango in a bowl with the remaining salsa ingredients and set aside to develop the flavours. Meanwhile, preheat the oven to 240°C (450°F) Gas 8.

Prick the duck skin all over with a fork and rub with a little salt. Transfer the duck breasts to a wire rack set over a roasting pan (this will allow the excess fat to drip away).

Put the soy sauce and honey into a small bowl and mix well. Spread the mixture over the duck skin. Transfer to the oven and roast for 15–20 minutes, until the duck is just cooked but still pink in the middle, and the skin well browned and crisp. Remove from the oven and let the duck rest for 5 minutes before carving.

Carve the duck breasts crossways into slices and serve with the mango salsa.

little chickens with citrus baked rice

This delicious dish of mini chicken and rice is a cross between a paella and a risotto, with the rice cooking and swelling in the hot stock in the oven. Cooking the poussins/Cornish game hens breast side down gives you a lovely, moist breast, as the fat and juices from the legs will seep down into it. You still get a crisp, golden skin, when you turn them back to breast side up for the last stage of cooking.

4 poussins/Cornish game hens
4 garlic cloves, crushed
4 bay leaves
leaves from 2 sprigs of rosemary
3 unwaxed lemons, halved crossways
150 ml/²⁄₃ cup white wine
4 tablespoons virgin olive oil
2 large Spanish onions, sliced
2 teaspoons turmeric
500 g/2¹⁄₃ cups risotto rice, such as arborio or carnaroli
about 1 litre/4 cups hot chicken stock
virgin olive oil, for roasting
salt and freshly ground black pepper

serves 4

Put the poussins/Cornish game hens in a large bowl and add plenty of salt and pepper. Rub with the garlic, sprinkle with the herbs, squeeze over the lemon juice and add the squeezed lemon halves to the bowl. Pour in the wine and half the oil. Cover and refrigerate for at least 2 hours, or overnight.

Preheat the oven to 200°C (400°F) Gas 6. Heat the remaining oil in a paella pan or large, heavy roasting pan. Add the onions and fry until softened. Add the turmeric and fry gently for 30 seconds. Add the rice and cook for 1 minute, stirring well.

Put the poussins/hens, breast side down, on top of the rice. Pour the marinade juices and half the hot stock over the top.

Bring to the boil on top of the stove, then remove from the heat and cover the whole pan with foil. Transfer to the preheated oven and cook for 25 minutes.

Remove from the oven and discard the foil. Turn the poussins/hens over and add the remaining stock to the pan. Brush the poussins/hens with a little extra oil. Return the uncovered pan to the oven and cook for a further 30 minutes until the poussins/hens and rice are cooked.

Note You may need to add extra stock to the pan if the rice starts to dry out. Check several times as it is cooking.

herbed seared lamb with
mediterranean vegetable purée

meat

Marinated, seared, roasted, stir-fried or grilled/broiled – the list is endless! Meat is a great, versatile ingredient. My tip is to spend more and buy less of the best quality you can find.

herbed seared lamb with mediterranean vegetable purée

Butterflying a leg of lamb opens it out flat, with no bones, to an even thickness. It's a good way to speed up the cooking time, and gives a larger surface area for searing and flavouring. Ask your butcher to butterfly the lamb for you.

1.8-kg/4-lb. leg of lamb, butterflied
8 garlic cloves, sliced
½ bottle red wine
3 tablespoons olive oil
grated zest of 1 lemon
2–3 sprigs of thyme
2–3 sprigs of rosemary
freshly ground black pepper

MEDITERRANEAN VEGETABLE BUTTER
2 medium aubergines/eggplant, cut into 1-cm/½-inch cubes
2 courgettes/zucchini, cut into 1-cm/½-inch cubes
5 tablespoons extra virgin olive oil
freshly squeezed lemon juice, to taste
salt and freshly ground black pepper

serves 4–6

Using a sharp knife, remove the excess fat and skin from the lamb. Cut small pockets into the flesh on both sides and stud each pocket with the garlic slices.

Put the wine, oil, lemon zest, thyme and rosemary in a large dish and sprinkle with pepper. Add the lamb, cover and refrigerate for at least 4 hours, preferably overnight.

Preheat the oven to 200°C (400°F) Gas 6. Put the aubergine/eggplant and courgette/zucchini cubes in a large roasting pan. Drizzle with 3 tablespoons of the oil and sprinkle with black pepper. Roast in the oven for 35–40 minutes until tender. Transfer to a plate and set aside. Reduce the oven temperature to 190°C (375°F) Gas 5.

Put the roasting pan over a high heat on top of the stove. Drain the lamb by tipping the marinade into a saucepan while you hold the lamb in the dish. Put the drained lamb in the hot roasting pan and sear for 5 minutes on each side to seal. Meanwhile, heat the marinade in the saucepan and boil for 2–3 minutes, to reduce. Pour the marinade over the lamb and top with the herb sprigs.

Transfer the lamb to the oven and roast for 20 minutes per 500 g/pound for medium lamb – check after 15 minutes per 500 g/pound for rare or after 25–30 minutes for well done. (Remember that thin pieces of meat will cook faster than thick ones – see page 79 for other roasting times.) Remove from the oven, cover with foil, and let rest for 10 minutes.

Put the vegetables and remaining oil into a food processor. Pulse to a coarse paste. Add salt, pepper, and lemon juice. Carve the lamb into thick slices and arrange on a platter. Serve with pan juices and the Mediterranean vegetable purée.

peppered sage pork with pasta

When cooking pork without crackling, always cook it gently, or it will become tough.

2 sun-dried peppers
500 g/1 lb. pork fillet/tenderloin
8 sage leaves
250 g/8 oz. pappardelle or tagliatelle pasta
15 g/1 tablespoon butter
½ tablespoon olive oil
4 tablespoons dry sherry
200 ml/¾ cup double/heavy cream
100 ml/½ cup chicken stock
1 tablespoon chopped fresh sage
salt and freshly ground black pepper

serves 4

Soak the sun-dried peppers in boiling water according to the manufacturer's instructions. Drain and cut into about 5-cm/2-inch pieces.

Slice the pork fillet/tenderloin diagonally into 8 pieces. Using the palm of your hand, gently flatten the pieces of pork into round, medallion shapes.

Using a small, sharp knife, make 2 cuts through the centre of each medallion. Thread a piece of sliced pepper through 1 cut and a sage leaf through the second cut of each medallion. Sprinkle with black pepper.

Cook the pasta in a saucepan of boiling, salted water, as directed on the package, until cooked, or "al dente".

Meanwhile, heat the butter and oil in a non-stick frying pan until foaming. Add the pork medallions and fry over a gentle to medium heat for 4–5 minutes on each side until golden and cooked all the way through. Transfer to a warm plate, cover with foil and set aside.

Pour the sherry into the hot frying pan and boil for 30 seconds. Stir in the cream, stock and sage. Bring to the boil again, reduce the heat and simmer for 3–4 minutes. Add salt and pepper to taste.

Drain the pasta, return it to the warm saucepan and toss with half of the sauce. Divide between serving plates. Top with 2 pieces of pork. Drizzle with the remaining sauce and serve at once.

chili con carne wraps

Adding the bitter dark chocolate at the last minute adds a lovely richness — as well as a dash of Mexican authenticity — to the sauce and brings it all together.

1 tablespoon olive oil, plus extra for brushing
1 large onion, chopped
2 teaspoons crushed dried chillies/hot red pepper flakes
400 g/14 oz. canned red kidney beans, drained and rinsed
400 g/14 oz. canned chopped tomatoes
150 ml/⅔ cup red wine
2 garlic cloves, crushed
4 flour tortillas
2 sirloin steaks, 250 g/8 oz. each
15 g/½ oz. dark/bittersweet chocolate (minimum 70 per cent cocoa solids), coarsely chopped
freshly ground black pepper
chilli/chili oil, to drizzle

TO SERVE
chunky guacamole (page 143)
150 ml/⅔ cup sour cream
½ iceberg lettuce, finely shredded

serves 4

Heat the oil in a large saucepan. Add the onion and fry for 5–6 minutes until golden. Stir in the dried chillies/pepper flakes, kidney beans, tomatoes, wine and garlic. Bring to the boil, reduce the heat and simmer for 15–20 minutes.

Heat a stove-top grill pan until very hot. Add the tortillas, one at a time, and cook for 1 minute on each side until lightly toasted. Put them in a very low oven to keep warm.

Brush the steaks with olive oil and sprinkle with freshly ground black pepper. Add the steaks to the grill pan and sear for 2–3 minutes on each side for medium rare, or about 1–2 minutes longer, depending on thickness, if you prefer your meat well done.

Remove from the pan and drizzle with the chilli/chili oil. Let the meat rest for 5 minutes before cutting into diagonal slices. Meanwhile, stir the chocolate into the sauce.

Serve as a wrap in the warm tortillas, with chunky guacamole, sour cream and lettuce.

lemongrass and rosemary risotto
with orange roasted roots

vegetables

You'll find lots of vegetable dishes throughout this book, but most of the recipes in this section treat them as a substantial course in themselves.

lemongrass and rosemary risotto with orange roasted roots

Always add liquid to a risotto gradually so that the rice absorbs it little by little, as it swells and cooks. The stock should go in hot, so put it in a saucepan over a low heat and ladle it in as you go.

2 tablespoons olive oil
1 large onion, finely chopped
1 stalk of lemongrass
a large sprig of rosemary, plus extra to serve
375 g/1¾ cups risotto rice, such as arborio or carnaroli
300 ml/1¼ cups white wine
about 850 ml/3¾ cups hot vegetable stock
1 tablespoon chopped fresh rosemary
salt and freshly ground black pepper
1 recipe orange roasted roots (page 84), to serve

serves 4

Put the oil into a large saucepan and heat. When hot, add the onion and fry for 5–8 minutes until softened and turning golden.

Using a rolling pin, lightly bruise the lemongrass and the sprig of rosemary to release the flavours. Add to the onion, then add the rice and cook, stirring continuously, for 1 minute.

Add the wine, 1 ladle of hot stock and salt and freshly ground black pepper to taste. Bring to the boil, then reduce the heat to simmering. As the stock is absorbed, gradually add more, 1 ladle at a time, letting each be absorbed before adding the next.

Cook for about 20 minutes, stirring frequently, until the rice is cooked through. Stir in the chopped rosemary and salt and pepper to taste.

Pile the risotto onto 4 large plates or bowls. Top with the hot root vegetables and a sprig of rosemary, then serve.

creamy scalloped potatoes and parsnips

This is one of my all-time favourites, and yes, it does need all that cream!

425 ml/1¾ cups double/heavy cream
300 ml/1¼ cups milk
2 garlic cloves, crushed
freshly grated nutmeg
1 bay leaf
500 g/1 lb. potatoes, finely sliced
500 g/1 lb. parsnips, finely sliced
salt and freshly ground black pepper
a shallow, medium ovenproof dish, lightly buttered

serves 4

Preheat the oven to 170°C (325°F) Gas 3. Put the cream, milk, garlic, nutmeg to taste and bay leaf into a saucepan with salt and pepper to taste. Heat gently to just below boiling point, then remove from the heat.

Arrange layers of potatoes and parsnips in the prepared dish. Pour in the cream mixture. Cover with foil and cook in the preheated oven for 45 minutes. Remove the foil and cook in the oven for about 30 minutes more, until golden.

mushroom, leek and
thyme puff pies

mushroom, leek and thyme puff pies

Add the cream cheese to the leeks and mushrooms only after they have cooled, or the cheese will melt and make the filling runny. Make sure you wash the leeks thoroughly, to remove any dirt or grit between the layers.

25 g/2 tablespoons butter
2 leeks, washed and finely sliced diagonally
250 g/8 oz. flat, open mushrooms, finely sliced
1 large garlic clove, crushed
200 g/1 scant cup cream cheese
flour, for dusting
2 tablespoons thyme leaves
375 g/13 oz. ready-rolled puff pastry
1 egg, beaten with a pinch of salt
salt and freshly ground black pepper

serves 4

Heat half the butter in a large frying pan or wok until melted. Add the leeks and fry for about 5 minutes until softened. Transfer to a large bowl.

Add the remaining butter to the frying pan and heat until melted. Add the mushrooms and garlic and cook for 5 minutes until softened and the juices have evaporated. Add to the leeks with plenty of salt and pepper and let cool. When completely cool, add the cream cheese and mix well.

Dust a work surface with flour and sprinkle with the thyme. Put the pastry on top of the thyme and roll out to a square, about 32 cm/12 inches. Turn the pastry over. Using a sharp knife, cut into 4 smaller squares.

Spoon the mixture onto one side of each square leaving a 1-cm/½-inch border at the edges. Brush the border with a little water, then fold the pastry over the filling. Press the edges lightly together and use the back of a fork to seal the edges. Brush with the beaten egg to glaze and then, using a sharp knife, cut a small slit in each to let air escape. Transfer to a baking sheet, cover and refrigerate for 30 minutes.

Meanwhile, preheat the oven to 200°C (400°F) Gas 6. Transfer the pies to the oven and bake for about 25–30 minutes until risen and golden brown.

VEGETABLE TIPS

- Buy small quantities and buy often.
- Don't keep tomatoes in the refrigerator – keep them at room temperature. Don't keep potatoes in the refrigerator either – keep them in a cool, dark place, such as a kitchen drawer or cupboard.
- Store other vegetables in the refrigerator to keep them fresh.
- When peeling most vegetables, use a peeler not a knife (though for hard-skinned vegetables like turnip, you will need a knife).
- When cutting vegetables to be boiled, cut into evenly-sized pieces so they will all be cooked at the same time – this is very important for broccoli, cauliflower and potatoes.
- Scrub organic vegetables well, but peel any that aren't organic.

vegetable goulash

Paprika gives Hungarian goulash its appealing reddish colour and fragrance. Here the smoked variety, often used in Spanish cookery, adds a distinctive, deep flavour.

2 tablespoons olive oil
1 large onion, chopped
1 big teaspoon brown sugar
3 garlic cloves, crushed
5 dried birdseye chillies/chiles, soaked in boiling water to cover
3 tablespoons smoked sweet paprika
1 large parsnip, cut into 2.5-cm/1-inch cubes
1 large potato, cubed
200 g/8 oz. baby carrots, trimmed and halved lengthways
800 g/3 cups canned chopped tomatoes
about 300 ml/1¼ cups red wine
410 g/14 oz. canned chickpeas, drained and rinsed
freshly ground black pepper

TO SERVE
2 tablespoons Greek yogurt or sour cream
a bunch of mint, coarsely chopped
lemon and cumin cracked wheat (right) or cooked rice (page 22)

serves 4

Put the oil in a large saucepan and heat. When hot, add the onions, cover with a lid and cook over medium heat for 10–15 minutes until softened. Remove the lid and stir in the sugar. Increase the heat to high and cook for a further 5 minutes until golden.

Add the garlic, drained chillies/chiles and paprika and cook for 30 seconds. Add all the vegetables, tomatoes and wine with 300 ml/1¼ cups water. Bring to the boil, reduce the heat and simmer, uncovered, for 35–40 minutes until the vegetables are just tender, adding a little extra water if they dry out. Add the chickpeas and plenty of black pepper and simmer for a further 5–10 minutes.

Transfer to serving plates and drizzle with the yogurt or sour cream. Sprinkle with the mint and serve with lemon and cumin cracked wheat or rice.

lemon and cumin cracked wheat

Cracked wheat is similar to bulgur wheat. Used often in Middle Eastern cookery, it is excellent served cold in salads or hot with chicken or vegetable dishes.

300 g/1 cup cracked wheat
2 tablespoons virgin olive oil
1 unwaxed lemon, finely chopped
3 teaspoons ground cumin
2 garlic cloves, crushed
freshly ground black pepper

serves 4

Put the cracked wheat in a bowl and add boiling water to cover. Allow to swell for 15–20 minutes until soft, then drain through a sieve/strainer, pressing out any excess water.

Heat the oil in a large saucepan. Add the lemon and fry for 2 minutes, then add the cumin and garlic and fry briefly for 30 seconds. Add the cracked wheat and stir-fry for a further 1–2 minutes. Add plenty of pepper, then serve.

vegetable goulash with lemon and cumin cracked wheat

luxury hummus

dressings, dips and sauces

Dips, dressings and sauces all bring a meal to life – so dip, dunk and mix away.

luxury hummus

You can really taste the difference in homemade hummus, especially this deluxe, caper-topped version.

1 can chickpeas, about 410 g/14 oz., drained and rinsed
3 tablespoons tahini paste
2 garlic cloves, coarsely chopped
freshly squeezed juice of 1 lemon
4 tablespoons extra virgin olive oil, plus extra to drizzle
a large bunch of flat leaf parsley, coarsely chopped
2 tablespoons capers, rinsed and drained
½ teaspoon crushed dried chillies/dried red pepper flakes
salt and freshly ground black pepper

TO SERVE
pita bread, toasted
1 lemon, cut into wedges

serves 4 as a starter/appetizer

Put the chickpeas, tahini paste and garlic in a food processor and blend until smooth. Add the lemon juice, with 3 tablespoons of the oil and 1 tablespoon boiling water. Process until very smooth. Add plenty of salt and black pepper.

Put the parsley, capers, dried chillies/pepper flakes and the remaining olive oil into a bowl and mix well.

Put a mound of the hummus on each toasted pita bread and top with a spoonful of the parsley-caper mixture. Drizzle with olive oil and serve with lemon wedges.

salsa verde

Salsa verde is a raw, green and extremely versatile sauce – great with fish and meat. This is just one of many variations.

50 g/2 cups wild rocket/arugula, coarsely chopped
½ bunch chives, coarsely chopped
4 tablespoons extra virgin olive oil
salt and freshly ground black pepper

serves 4

Put the rocket/arugula in a blender, add the chives, olive oil and 2 tablespoons water. Blend until smooth. Add salt and pepper to taste, then serve. Refrigerate for up to 1 day.

Note If you don't have a regular, bench-top blender, a small, inexpensive stick blender is fine.

chunky guacamole

Use avocados which are just ripe – overripe ones taste bitter and rancid.

2 large ripe avocados, halved, pitted, peeled and cut into 1-cm/½-inch cubes
freshly squeezed juice of 1 lime
2 shallots, finely chopped
8 cherry tomatoes, quartered
1 large red chilli/chile, seeded and finely chopped (page 43)
1 garlic clove, finely chopped
a pinch of sugar
1 tablespoon extra virgin olive oil
salt and freshly ground black pepper

serves 4

Put the avocado in a bowl and pour over the lime juice. Add the remaining ingredients to the bowl with a little salt and lots of freshly ground black pepper. Mix well.

To serve as a starter/appetizer, fill 4 teacups with the relish and turn them out into a mound on the centre of each serving plate. Drizzle with oil and sprinkle with black pepper.

fresh red pepper jam

pimento paste

fresh red pepper jam

Superb with pasta or on top of toasted bread with shavings of cheese.

2 tablespoons olive oil

2 red (bell) peppers, halved, seeded and finely sliced

2 yellow (bell) peppers, halved, seeded and finely sliced

2 orange (bell) peppers, halved, seeded and finely sliced

1 red chilli/chile, halved, seeded (page 43) and finely sliced diagonally

2 garlic cloves, peeled

1 tablespoon sugar

1 lemon, halved

salt and freshly ground black pepper

serves 4

Heat the oil in a large saucepan. Add the (bell) peppers, chilli/chile, garlic and sugar. Squeeze the lemon juice into the pan, then add the squeezed halves. Stir.

Put a piece of wet, crumpled greaseproof paper on top of the mixture in the pan and cover with a lid. Cook gently over a low heat for 35–40 minutes until the (bell) peppers are

STERILIZING JARS

Put the jars in a saucepan and fill the pan with water to cover the jars. Bring to the boil, reduce the heat slightly and boil gently for 10 minutes. Remove and let drain on kitchen paper/paper towels until dry.

meltingly soft. Remove the paper from the pan and increase the heat to reduce the liquid for about 3–4 minutes. Add salt and pepper to taste and remove from the heat. When cool, transfer to sterilized jars (below). Keep refrigerated and use within 1–2 weeks.

quick aïoli

A short-cut, easy version of this garlic flavoured mayonnaise.

2 garlic cloves, crushed

6 tablespoons mayonnaise

2 tablespoons crème fraîche or Greek yogurt

2 tablespoons flat leaf parsley, chopped

salt and freshly ground black pepper

serves 4

Put the ingredients in a bowl and stir to mix. Keep refrigerated and use within 2 days.

pimento paste

Based on the classic French *rouille*, traditionally served with fish soup.

2 large red (bell) peppers

1 tablespoon olive oil

25 g/1 oz. white bread, crusts removed, soaked in a little water and excess squeezed out

2 garlic cloves, crushed

1 teaspoon cayenne pepper

100 ml/½ cup extra virgin olive oil

salt and freshly ground black pepper

serves 4

Preheat the oven to 200°C (400°F) Gas 6. Put the (bell) peppers in a roasting pan and drizzle with the oil.

Roast in the oven for 35–40 minutes, turning them occasionally, until slightly blackened all over. Put the (bell) peppers in a large plastic food bag, seal and let cool. The steam released will loosen the skins.

Remove the (bell) peppers from the bag, reserving any juices. Peel off the skin, cut in half and remove the seeds. Put the (bell) pepper halves in a food processor with the bread, garlic, cayenne and pepper juices and blend until smooth. With the motor running, slowly add the olive oil. Add salt and black pepper to taste. Keep refrigerated and use within 2 days.

red onion marmalade

Delicious in burgers, with sausages and cold meat, or on bruschetta with goat cheese (page 64).

2 tablespoons olive oil
750 g/1½ lbs. red onions,
   very thinly sliced
1 bay leaf
1 teaspoon thyme leaves
50 g/¼ cup Demerara/brown sugar
3 tablespoons balsamic vinegar
150 ml/⅔ cup red wine
grated zest and juice of 1 orange
salt and freshly ground black pepper

serves 8

Heat the oil in a large saucepan until hot. Add the onions, bay leaf and thyme and salt and black pepper to taste. Cover with a lid and cook over a low heat, stirring occasionally, for 30 minutes until the onions are softened and translucent.

Add the sugar, vinegar, red wine and the orange zest and juice. Cook uncovered for a further 1½ hours until no liquid is left and the onions are a dark, rich, red colour. Stir frequently during the last 30 minutes to stop the onions burning.

Let the mixture cool, then transfer to sterilized jars (see opposite). It will keep refrigerated for several weeks.

roquefort sauce

Wonderful as a dip with celery and breadsticks, on burgers or with chicken cooked in the grill pan.

100 g/4 oz. Roquefort cheese
200 g/1 cup Greek yogurt
freshly ground black pepper

serves 4

Put the Roquefort in a bowl and coarsely crush with a fork. Stir in the yogurt and sprinkle with black pepper. If the yogurt is quite thick, you can add 1–2 tablespoons of cold water.

lemon beurre blanc

A lighter, lemon version of the classic French butter sauce – perfect with fish.

2 shallots, finely chopped
4 black peppercorns
2 parsley stalks
250 ml/1 cup white wine
1 tablespoon white wine vinegar
6 tablespoons double/heavy cream
50 g/4 tablespoons unsalted butter,
   diced and chilled
freshly squeezed lemon juice
salt and freshly ground black pepper

serves 4

Put the shallots, peppercorns, parsley stalks, wine and vinegar in a medium saucepan. Bring to the boil, reduce the heat and simmer until the mixture has reduced by half. Add the cream and simmer for 1–2 minutes.

Reduce the heat to very low and gently whisk in the chilled butter. Pass the sauce through a sieve/strainer and add salt, pepper and lemon juice to taste. Keep it warm until needed.

dijon dressing

A simple all-purpose dressing for salads. You can adjust this as much as you like – try wholegrain mustard in place of smooth, and experiment with different vinegars – sherry, cider, red wine or even Japanese rice vinegar.

1 tablespoon smooth Dijon mustard
1 tablespoon white wine vinegar
4 tablespoons extra virgin olive oil
1 garlic clove, crushed
salt and freshly ground black pepper

serves 4

Put the mustard, vinegar, oil and garlic in a bowl and mix with a fork or small metal whisk. Add enough water for the consistency you want – about 1–2 tablespoons – and salt and black pepper to taste.

dijon dressing

sweet things

I think there's nothing to beat a homemade dessert – everyone loves them and making something simple and delicious can be very easy and quick.

mini pavlovas with hot sugared plums

Pavlova is a type of meringue, with a gooey middle that you get by adding cornflour and vinegar to regular meringue mixture. Traditionally, the meringue case is filled with cream and fresh fruit, but hot plums and ice cream make a fabulous variation. I also think it is more fun to serve little individual ones, which look prettier. You can make the meringue part up to a day in advance.

PAVLOVAS
3 egg whites
175 g/generous ¾ cup (caster) sugar
1 teaspoon cornflour/cornstarch
½ teaspoon white wine vinegar

PLUMS
500 g/1 lb. plums, about 8, halved and pitted
1 teaspoon ground cinnamon
40 g/3 tablespoons (caster) sugar
15 g/1 tablespoon butter

TO SERVE
vanilla ice cream
4 sprigs of mint
a baking sheet, lined with parchment paper

serves 4

Preheat the oven to 140°C (275°F) Gas 1.

Put the egg whites into a clean bowl and, using an electric whisk, whisk until stiff. Gradually whisk in the sugar, until the mixture is very stiff. Sift in the cornflour/cornstarch, then, using a large metal spoon, fold in with the vinegar.

Divide the mixture into 4 mounds on the parchment. Using a dessert spoon, flatten to a disc shape, making a light indent in the middle of each. Bake in the preheated oven for about 30–40 minutes until the meringue is hard and the baking parchment peels away from the bottom of the pavlovas. Cool on a wire rack. You can make these up to 1 day in advance and store them in an airtight container.

Increase the oven to 200°C (400°F) Gas 6. Put the plums, cut side up, on a baking sheet. Put the cinnamon and sugar in a bowl, mix and sprinkle over the plums. Divide the butter between the plums, transfer to the oven and bake for 15–20 minutes until golden and bubbling hot.

Put the pavlovas onto small plates and top with a few scoops of vanilla ice cream. Put the hot plums beside the pavlovas and decorate with mint.

peach marsala trifle

Based on Italian tiramisù, with the added bonus of plenty of fruit. No jelly in sight!

300 ml/1¼ cups strong black coffee
200 ml/¾ cup Marsala wine
115 g/3 oz. sponge fingers/ladyfingers
4 ripe peaches or nectarines, halved and pitted
250 g/1 cup mascarpone cheese
25 g/2 tablespoons (caster) sugar
300 ml/1¼ cups double/heavy cream
cocoa powder, for dusting

serves 6

Put the coffee and 150 ml/⅔ cup of the Marsala into a shallow serving dish. Dip each sponge finger/ladyfinger into the coffee mixture and use to line the base of the dish. Cut the peaches or nectarines into thin slices and arrange in layers over the sponge fingers/ladyfingers.

Put the mascarpone and sugar into a large bowl and beat with a wooden spoon until soft. Gently beat in the cream and the remaining Marsala.

Spoon the mascarpone mixture over the peaches and, using a spatula, smooth to cover the fruit. Dust generously with cocoa powder. Cover and refrigerate for 2 hours to let the flavours soak into each other, then serve.

peach marsala trifle

cherry almond tart

cherry almond tart

Canned Morello cherries have a wonderful sweet-sour flavour, but fresh cherries or ripe, sliced nectarines are a good substitute if you can't find them. The preheated baking sheet gives a crisp base, as its even heat cooks the pastry from underneath.

375 g/13 oz. ready-to-roll sweet or shortcrust pastry
100 g/7 tablespoons unsalted butter
100 g/½ cup (caster) sugar
2 eggs, beaten
2 tablespoons brandy
100 g/1 cup ground almonds
2 tablespoons plain/all-purpose flour
350 g/1 cup canned Morello cherries, drained
icing/confectioners' sugar, for dusting
double/heavy cream or vanilla ice cream, to serve
a fluted tart pan, 25 cm/10 inches diameter
a baking sheet

serves 6–8

Put a baking sheet in the oven and preheat to 200°C (400°F) Gas 6.

Roll out the pastry to just bigger than the tart pan. Carefully roll it around the rolling pin and drape over the tart pan. Press the pastry gently into the pan and, using a knife, trim off any pastry hanging over the edges. Prick the base lightly with a fork, then cover and refrigerate.

Meanwhile, put the butter and sugar in a bowl. Using an electric whisk, beat until pale and creamy. Gradually beat in the eggs, then stir in the brandy, almonds and flour.

Spread the mixture evenly over the pastry case and gently push the cherries at regular intervals into the surface. Put the tart onto the preheated baking sheet in the oven and bake for 10–15 minutes until the pastry begins to turn golden. Reduce the oven temperature to 180°C (350°F) Gas 4 and continue baking for a further 30–35 minutes until golden and cooked.

Let cool slightly, then remove from the pan and dust lightly with icing/confectioners' sugar. Cut into wedges and serve with cream or ice cream.

CHEAT'S PASTRY

• Supermarkets sell most kinds of pastry in ready-to-roll form — either chilled or frozen.
• Use sweet shortcrust pastry for sweet pies and all the other kinds of pastry for just about anything.

hot tropical fruit packages

If you fancy a kick of alcohol, add a spoonful of white rum to each package before sealing and baking.

2 large oranges
2 large ripe mangoes
4 passionfruit
4 teaspoons (caster) sugar
1 lime, quartered lengthways
coconut and lime ice cream (page 150) or vanilla ice cream, to serve
4 rectangles of foil, 30 x 20 cm/12 x 8 inches each

serves 4

Preheat the oven to 200°C (400°F) Gas 6. Split the oranges into segments over a bowl, catching any juice in the bowl. Cut chunks from the mango and peel off the skin. Cut the passionfruit in half and scoop out the pulp. Add the sugar, mango chunks, orange segments and passionfruit pulp to the bowl and mix gently.

Divide the fruit between the foil rectangles, spooning over the remaining juice. Top each with a lime quarter. Scrunch the foil together to seal and transfer to a baking sheet. Cook in the oven for 6–8 minutes.

Put each package on a plate for everyone to open their own. Serve the ice cream separately.

coconut and lime ice cream

You don't need an ice cream maker to make ice cream, just an ordinary freezer and a shallow container. If your ice cream is rock solid, transfer it from the freezer to the refrigerator twenty minutes before serving so that it can soften slightly.

425 ml/2½ cups canned coconut cream
4 egg yolks
115 g/generous ½ cup (caster) sugar
grated zest of 2 limes

serves 4

Put the coconut cream into a non-stick saucepan over medium heat. Heat slowly to just below boiling point, then remove from the heat.

Meanwhile, put the egg yolks and sugar into a bowl and, using an electric whisk, whisk until pale and thick.

Slowly pour the hot coconut cream into the egg mixture, whisking continuously.

Wipe out the saucepan with kitchen paper/paper towels and pour in the coconut and egg mixture. Return to medium heat and cook very gently, stirring continuously with a wooden spoon, until it thickens. Make sure it doesn't boil, or the mixture will curdle.

Pour into a bowl and let cool to room temperature.

Stir the lime zest into the cooled mixture, then pour into an ice cream maker and churn until frozen. If you don't have an ice cream maker, pour the mixture into a shallow metal or plastic container and put it into the freezer until half frozen, then remove from the freezer, whisk and return it to the freezer until solid.

hot whisky crêpes with raspberries

You can make the crêpes for this heartwarming dessert ahead of time — keep them in the refrigerator for up to two days, separated by squares of greaseproof paper. Alternatively, freeze them once they have cooled and remove from the freezer thirty minutes before using.

55 g/generous ¼ cup plain/all-purpose flour
a pinch of salt
1 egg
150 ml/⅔ cup milk
2 teaspoons peanut oil
300 ml/1¼ cups freshly squeezed orange juice
2 tablespoons honey
15 g/1 tablespoon butter
3 tablespoons whisky
175 g/1¼ cups fresh raspberries
icing/confectioners' sugar, to dust
cream or Greek yogurt, to serve

serves 4

Sift the flour and salt into a large bowl. Make a well in the centre and crack the egg into the well. Gradually whisk in the milk to form a smooth batter.

Heat a medium, non-stick frying pan. Add a little oil and wipe out with kitchen paper/paper towels. Pour enough batter into the pan to coat the base, then cook for about 1 minute. Loosen the edges with a long-handled turner, flip the crêpe and cook for 1 minute more. Transfer to a plate and repeat with the remaining mixture to make 3 more crêpes. Set aside.

Pour the orange juice into the frying pan and add the honey and butter. Bring to the boil, reduce the heat and simmer for 5 minutes to concentrate the flavours and thicken the sauce slightly. Stir in the whisky.

Carefully fold each crêpe in half, then in half again to make a triangle, and slide them into the simmering sauce. Heat for 30 seconds to warm through.

Transfer the crêpes and sauce to a serving plate and sprinkle with raspberries. Dust lightly with icing/confectioners' sugar and serve with cream or Greek yogurt.

FRESH FRUIT FOR DESSERT

• Remember that fresh fruit makes a quick and easy end to a meal, even something as simple as orange wedges.

• In Greece, chunks and slices of fresh fruit are arranged in a dish of crushed ice and lime or lemon juice squeezed over the top.

• Prepare fruit in easily manageable sizes and keep it casual — life's too short to learn how to eat a grape with a knife and fork!

• Some fruits turn brown when exposed to air — apples and pears for instance. To stop this, brush the cut surfaces with lemon juice.

hot whisky crêpes with raspberries

pecan mocha brownies

Brownies make an easy pudding. Serve them warm, straight from the oven, with a dollop of extra thick cream and a handful of raspberries. Alternatively, let them cool and eat them any time of day. Don't overcook brownies – they should be slightly gooey in the middle.

115 g/1 stick unsalted butter
170 g/generous ¾ cup (caster) sugar
1 teaspoon vanilla extract
2 eggs, beaten
55 g/⅓ cup plain/all-purpose flour
55 g/½ cup cocoa powder
1 teaspoon baking powder
55 g/⅓ cup pecans, coarsely chopped
40 g/1½ oz. dark/bittersweet chocolate (minimum 70 per cent cocoa solids), coarsely chopped
2 teaspoons instant coffee, dissolved in 2 tablespoons boiling water
a cake pan, 18 cm/8 inches square, greased, lined with greaseproof paper and lightly buttered

makes 9

Preheat the oven to 180°C (350°F) Gas 4.

Put the butter and sugar into a large bowl and, using an electric whisk, beat together until pale and fluffy. Add the vanilla and gradually beat in the eggs.

Sift the flour, cocoa powder and baking powder into the butter mixture and, using a large metal spoon, gently fold to mix. Fold in the pecans, chocolate and coffee. Spoon the mixture into the prepared pan and level out the top with the back of the spoon.

Transfer to the preheated oven and bake for about 30–35 minutes until just firm on top. If you are not eating the brownies immediately, leave in the pan for 10 minutes, then remove from the pan and transfer to a wire rack to cool. Cut into squares and serve.

brandied truffle curls

You need to make these quickly, while the mixture is still quite firm from the refrigerator. But don't be too precious – they look much better if they aren't all perfect!

200 g/7 oz. dark/bittersweet chocolate (minimum 70 per cent cocoa solids), coarsely chopped
150 ml/⅔ cup double/heavy cream
2 tablespoons brandy or whisky
55 g/4 tablespoons unsalted butter, softened (room temperature)
25 g/¼ cup cocoa powder

makes about 30

Put the chocolate and cream in a heatproof bowl set over a saucepan of simmering water and gently heat until the chocolate is just melted. Remove from the heat and stir in the brandy or whisky. Set aside for 5 minutes, then beat in the butter. Let cool, then transfer to the refrigerator and leave until the mixture has slightly hardened.

Sift the cocoa powder onto a plate. Draw a teaspoon across the truffle mixture, pressing slightly to pick up the mixture in the scoop of the spoon and to form curls. Dip them into the sifted cocoa, put on a large serving plate and refrigerate until needed.

hot chocolate fondue

A fabulous dipping sauce, as well as an excellent hot topping for ice cream. Alternatively, let it cool and thicken and spread it between two layers of vanilla cake.

200 g/7 oz. dark/bittersweet chocolate, coarsely chopped
40 g/3 tablespoons unsalted butter
150 ml/⅔ cup double/heavy cream
3 tablespoons brandy
150 ml/⅔ cup boiling water

FOR DIPPING
4 baby bananas, peeled
1 small pineapple, peeled and cut into chunks
125 g/1 cup black grapes
2 ripe pears, cut into slices
250 g/2 cups large strawberries
1 loaf brioche bread or small panettone, cut into 3-cm/1-inch cubes

serves 4

Put the chocolate, butter and cream into a heatproof bowl set over a saucepan of simmering water. Gently heat until melted and smooth. Remove from the heat and stir in the brandy and water. Transfer to a fondue pot or warm saucepan. Serve with fruits and breads for dipping.

drinks

Hot and frothy, long and cool and some with a bit of a kick! This chapter has drinks for every occasion – try a brandied hot chocolate on your own, or round up your friends for a big, cold jug of Sea Breeze or Sangría.

very berry smoothie

The Greek yogurt in this bright, summery smoothie adds a creamy taste and colour to the red berries. Add more or less honey, depending on how sweet you like your smoothies.

125 g/1 cup strawberries, hulled
125 g/1 cup raspberries
50 g/½ cup blueberries
200 ml/¾ cup cranberry juice
4 tablespoons Greek yogurt
1 teaspoon (runny) honey
4 large ice cubes

serves 2

Put 2 tall glasses in the freezer to chill.

Put all the ingredients in a blender or food processor and work until almost smooth. Taste for sweetness, adding more honey if needed. Pour into the 2 chilled glasses and serve immediately.

tropical smoothie

Try to find a ripe and juicy mango to make this smoothie – it should be really fragrant. Peeling and slicing mangoes is quite a messy process, but absolutely worth it!

1 ripe mango
1 ripe banana, coarsely chopped
grated zest and juice of 1 lime
60 ml/⅓ cup freshly squeezed orange juice

serves 2

To slice the mango, cut off both sides of the fruit either side of the stone/seed. Peel back the skin and, at the same time, scoop out the flesh with a spoon. Cut into slices. Peel off the remaining skin from the mango and, using a knife, cut as much flesh as you can from the stone/seed.

Put the bananas, mango slices, lime zest and juice and orange juice in a blender or food processor and work until smooth. Pour into glasses and serve at once.

irish coffee

8 tablespoons Irish whiskey
4 teaspoons light muscovado/brown sugar
1 cafetière of fresh hot coffee (4-cup size)
150 ml/⅔ cup double/heavy cream, lightly whipped
white chocolate truffles, to serve (optional)

serves 4

Put 2 tablespoons whiskey and 1 teaspoon sugar in each cup and stir. Add the hot coffee and stir briefly. Top with a generous spoonful of the cream and serve immediately, with chocolate truffles, if using.

amaretto iced cappuccino

A deluxe version of iced coffee, with a shot of Amaretto liqueur to make it extra special. Dunk the biscotti and let them soak up the creamy, almondy, coffee flavours.

4 scoops good-quality vanilla ice cream
300 ml/1¼ cups espresso coffee, freshly brewed
4 tablespoons Amaretto liqueur
biscotti cookies, to serve

serves 2

Divide the vanilla ice cream between two extra large coffee cups. Put the coffee and Amaretto in a jug/cup, mix, then pour over the ice cream. Serve immediately with the biscotti.

café frappé

Iced coffee really hits the spot on hot summer days, when you need a boost of caffeine as well as a refreshing, cool and creamy drink.

1 cafetière of fresh coffee (4-cup size), cooled
2 tablespoons (caster) sugar
150 ml/⅔ cup double/heavy or single/light cream
4 tablespoons milk

serves 2

Pour the cooled coffee into an ice-cube tray, put in the freezer and freeze until almost solid.

Put the coffee ice cubes in a food processor with the sugar and process until coarsely chopped. Add the cream and milk and process until very finely chopped. Add more sugar as needed. Serve immediately in tall, chilled glasses.

brandied hot chocolate

The ultimate winter indulgence! One to sip from the comfort of a big armchair in front of a glowing fire.

250 ml/1 cup milk
45 g/2 oz. dark/bittersweet chocolate (minimum 70 per cent cocoa solids), grated
1 teaspoon sugar
2 tablespoons brandy
lightly whipped double/heavy cream, to serve (optional)

serves 1

Put the milk in a saucepan and heat to just below boiling point. Add the chocolate and sugar and stir over a very low heat until the chocolate has melted. Stir in the brandy and then pour into a mug. Finish with a spoonful of cream, if desired.

sea breeze

200 ml/1 cup vodka
500 ml/2 cups cranberry juice
300 ml/1¼ cups grapefruit juice
ice cubes
1 lime, cut into wedges, to serve

serves 4

Put the vodka, cranberry juice and grapefruit juice into a large jug/pitcher and mix well. Half fill 4 large glasses with ice, then pour the mixture over the ice. Top with a wedge of lime and serve immediately.

margarita

1 lime, cut into 6 wedges
coarsely ground salt
250 ml/1 cup best quality tequila
75 ml/⅓ cup Cointreau or Triple Sec
150 ml/⅔ cup freshly squeezed lime juice, about 5–6 limes
3–4 tablespoons sugar, or to taste

serves 4

To salt-rim the glasses, rub a lime wedge around the rim of each glass. Put the salt on a small plate and dip each glass into the salt. Freeze until needed.

Pour the tequila, Cointreau, lime juice and sugar into a blender or food processor half-filled with ice. Process until the ice is finely chopped and the mixture becomes frothy. Taste for sweetness, adding more sugar if necessary. Pour into the chilled glasses and serve with a wedge of lime.

sangría

1 bottle rosé wine, 750 ml
600 ml/2¾ cups (cloudy) lemonade
600 ml/2¾ cups freshly squeezed orange juice
freshly squeezed juice of 2 lemons
150 ml/⅔ cup brandy
2 oranges, sliced or cut into small wedges
2 lemons, sliced or cut into small wedges
ice cubes, to serve

serves 6–8

Put the wine, lemonade, orange juice, lemon juice and brandy into a very large jug/pitcher or 2 small ones and mix. Add the orange and lemon slices and top up with plenty of ice. Serve in large, chilled wine glasses.

bloody mary

200 ml/1 cup vodka
850 ml/3¾ cups tomato juice
2 teaspoons horseradish sauce (optional)
1 tablespoon Tabasco, or to taste
2 tablespoons Worcestershire sauce
1 teaspoon celery salt
freshly ground black pepper

TO SERVE
ice cubes
4 celery stalks
1 lemon, cut into 4 wedges

serves 4

Put all the ingredients in a large jug/pitcher and mix. Add black pepper to taste. Pour into 4 large glasses half filled with ice. Serve with a stalk of celery and a wedge of lemon.

index